Pennsylvania Literary Journal
Volume X, Issue 2
Summer 2018

Anna Faktorovich

Anaphora Literary Press

Quanah, Texas

EDITOR-IN-CHIEF

ANNA FAKTOROVICH

EDITORIAL BOARD

NICHOLAS BIRNS • DOUGLAS J. KING
ROBERT HAUPTMAN • WILLIAM IRWIN

ANAPHORA LITERARY PRESS
https://anaphoraliterary.com
director@anaphoraliterary.com
1108 W 3rd Street
Quanah, TX 79252

Book design by Anna Faktorovich, Ph.D.

Cover Image: "Poor Artist's Cupboard" by Charles Bird King (1815), oil on wood; Corcoran Collection (Museum Purchase, Gallery Fund and exchange): National Gallery of Art.

Published in 2018 by Anaphora Literary Press

Anna Faktorovich—1st edition.

ISSN: 2151-3066

Faktorovich, Anna, 1981-, editor.
    Pennsylvania Literary Journal : Volume X, Issue 2 / Anna Faktorovich
    220 p. ; 9 in.
    ISBN 978-1-68114-475-7 (softcover : alk. paper)
    ISBN 978-1-68114-476-4 (hardcover : alk. paper)
1. Literary Criticism—Comparative Literature.
2. Poetry—Anthologies (multiple authors). 3. Fiction—Fantasy—Short Stories.
PN1-9: Literary Periodicals; PN80-99: Literature Criticism
801 Philosophy & theory; 805 Serial publications

TABLE OF CONTENTS

INTRODUCTION / Anna Faktorovich   **5**

BOOK REVIEWS / Anna Faktorovich   **6**

ESSAY

R. Joseph Rodríguez / In the Antropoetas and Muses We Trust: 57
Reading and Teaching the Poetics about the Borderlands and Chi-
huahuan Desert

POETRY

Jonathan Bracker
    Cheerful, and Its Alternative   86
    Two Views of Away   87
    Into Later Life   88
    When It Is Time to Get Up   89
    That Old Gang of Mine   90
Michael Ceraolo / Five from Eighty Days
    July 19, 1881   91
    July 20, 1881   92
    July 21, 1881   93
    July 22, 1881   94
    July 23, 1881   95
Louis Gallo
    Wittgenstein: A Micro-Biography   96
    The Charm of Fine Manners   97
    Thales   98
    Scherzo Furiant—America Now   99
    Linguistics   100
    Latin   101
    Sprocket   103
    Hauntology: Origin   105
    Fyodor   106
    Ergo Sum   107
    Archetypes   109
Susie Gharib
    Beyond Repair   111
    Plaintive   112
    A Dormant Door Mat   114
    A Lateen Sail   115

Rob Luke
The Reckoning of Rabbit 117
Tom McFadden
Sharing Rain 119
Note-Ride 121
The Night Is a Poem 122
Andrew Alexander Mobbs
What Happens When the Sun Dies 124
Habitable Worlds That Have No Sun 127
Lessons from an Orca: Tonic Immobility 129
Lessons from a Bottlenose Dolphin: Echolocation 130
What Crosses the Mind of a Bird in a Storm 131
Timothy Robbins
Happy at Last 133
Fußball 134
The Informer 135
Inside Outside 136
Judy 137
Robert Ronnow
Rhodora in Winter 139
Peace Out 140
Ricardo's Lunch 141
Kobina Wright
Ujima 142
Ujamaa 144
Nia 146

SHORT STORIES

Dreadful Awakening / **John W. Dennehy** 147
Frannie Potter / **Alan Fleishman** 158
Shipmates / **Kevin Harris** 185
Baba Yaga, the Intersex Witch / **Kathleen Murphey** 210

Contributors *215*

INTRODUCTION

Anna Faktorovich, PhD

The content of this issue includes an extended set of detailed reviews from the editor, Anna Faktorovich, of recently released and forthcoming scholarly and general interest non-fiction books. These titles cover the history of the Americas, recent political issues and politicians, biographies of famous or applauded individuals, space exploration studies or personal narratives, and various other works (some outstanding and some nonsensical). Then follows a scholarly essay by R. Joseph Rodríguez, a professor at the California State University, Fresno, on reading and teaching poetics about the Borderlands. This season brought in an unusually heavy volume of innovative, modern and emotional poetry from Jonathan Bracker, Michael Ceraolo, Louis Gallo (a regular contributor, who offered eleven poems and all of them were too good to refuse), Susie Gharib, Rob Luke, Tom McFadden, Andrew Alexander Mobbs, Timothy Robbins, Robert Ronnow, and Kobina Wright. In the last section, you will find a set of short fictional stories on topics ranging from the sea to Eastern European fairytales from John W. Dennehy, Alan Fleishman, Kevin Harris and Kathleen Murphey.

The *Pennsylvania Literary Journal* is always actively inviting submissions in a variety of genres and modes. If you have a project you would like to share email it to Anna Faktorovich at director@anaphoraliterary.com.

BOOK REVIEWS

Anna Faktorovich, PhD

Answers to Random and Curious Questions About Space Exploration

Clayton C. Anderson. *It's a Question of Space: An Ordinary Astronaut's Answers to Sometimes Extraordinary Questions.* $16.95. 224pp, 6X9", 38 images. ISBN: 978-1-49620508-7. Lincoln: Nebraska University Press, July 1, 2018.

****

I read this book cover-to-cover as part of my research for my first science fiction novel. If I was not working on this book, it would have been difficult to get through all of these questions because they are so scattered. There are chapters that slightly break up the topics into the "Life of an Astronaut", "The International Space Station", "Philosophy and Politics" and the like, but frequently the same topic reappears not only within the same section, but also in other parts of the book. It would have been a much more helpful book, if the author wrote a textbook on how the body, objects and the like are affected by space flight, with sections on how to operate, build and otherwise organize a spaceship. It seems unlikely that there is a comprehensive multi-disciplinary book about how the human body reacts to space, how chemistry works in, how spaceships are engineered and the like. Each of these topics is typically handled separately. While this imaginary book is on my wish list, this current real publication does a pretty good job of addressing many of the curious aspects of spaceflight in a single source.

In it Clayton C. Anderson, a recently retired astronaut who is a long-time aerospace engineering lecturer, answers questions he has received from the general public online over the years. Anderson offers a lot of insights in part because he has spent a very long time in space in comparison with an average astronaut, 150 days on just one tour of the International Space Station. While I would have preferred more scientific and technological explanations, it was enjoyable to read a book spiced with Clayton's humor (I think I giggled a couple of times; I don't usually sympathize with American humor).

In reading this book, I was searching for clues on what it would be like for an alien species to live for decades in a weightless spaceship traveling through the vacuum of empty space between solar systems. By reading the whole book, I found bits of information, but there are too many summaries because each answer assumes no familiarity with the rest of the content of the book as they are the isolated replies Clayton gave to a specific query. For example on page 10, he summarizes that prior to launch he was trained in the "Russian systems (i.e., how to poop and pee, eat, and sleep in their kayuta...", and then he covers each of these in more detail as questions specifically about poop or sleep come up. When he does zoom in closely on specific tasks in space, the text is particularly interesting (at least for my research project). For example, when answering how one gets "dressed in space", he explains that one has to be "pulling your head through the rubber gasket-lined metal hole that attaches to your space helmet" with a "level of physical exertion that can cause the puking fit..." Then, he comments that it was also particularly difficult to put on shoes, but that they weren't necessary and that he typically went around shoeless (14). To place readers more fully into space in fiction, these types of details really help writers. Most of science fiction has characters in full gravitational pull in space rather than weightless and otherwise skims over the realities of spaceflight perhaps because there have previously been few books like this that zoom into these details.

A pleasant and insightful read for any fan of spaceflight as well as for researchers of space exploration (including rocket scientists). There is enough structure to the replies to take the reader on an exciting, dramatic narrative into space without taking on personal risk of exposure to radiation or potential death from all sorts of space-related disasters (explained herein).

New Curious Research on Exoplanets

Donald Goldsmith. *Exoplanets: Hidden Worlds and the Quest for Ex-*

traterrestrial Life. $24.95. 256pp, 6X9", 18 images. ISBN: 978-0674-97690-0. Cambridge: Harvard University Press, September, 2018.

****

This was another book that helped with my science fiction research. The likes of it was not available until this point because exoplanets have only recently been able to discover exoplanets and to learn about their rotation, chemistry and other components from observing their stars or watching them pass in front of a star. Most of previous science fiction has described worlds that are very similar to earth and creatures on them that have two arms, two legs, and two eyes just like humans. This book and others like it help to dispel these myths with the introduction of numerous other possible worlds on which life could conceivably dwell. Life can survive in the goldilocks zone where liquid water is present, but perhaps it can survive in colder or hotter climates as well, or perhaps a large planet or moon can create enough internal heat even if it is much further from the sun than earth is. These and various other topics related to exoplanets in other solar systems are covered across this interesting, relatively brief study. Every science fiction writer should read this book and others like it as without these realities, the human mind cannot stretch beyond our atmospheric and other conditions on Earth.

The book is neatly organized into chapters on scientific concepts such as cosmic distances, the history of previous unsuccessful searches for exoplanets, the history of the current breakthrough into measuring radial velocity to find planets, as well as various other approaches to this search. The book covers this topic in depth, but in a way that is approachable to the general reader. There are plenty of diagrams that show how measurements are taken, as well as graphs that explain relationships and patterns. I really enjoyed reading about the details of unique planets that have been discovered to gather data on the types of worlds aliens might live in. For example, Goldsmith describes a star, HD 209458, which has a "radius about 14 percent larger" than our sun, with a planet, Osiris, around it which has "diameter... 1.4 times Jupiter's", and amass "220 times the Earth's" (104). Other details about the likely temperatures on a planet like this as well as its chemical composition really start to paint what it would look like on its surface or in its oceans, or in its air. A table of the properties of the "Seven Trappist-1 Planets" also really paint the conditions on a whole solar system, to allow a reader to roam through these worlds and imagine their diversity and potential interplay. In other parts, there are discussions about interesting topics like the fact that young suns can be erratic and can suddenly collapse and explode.

This is not a textbook for an introductory astronomy class, but rather a book for a more advanced astronomy course for undergraduate or graduate students specifically interested in exoplanets. Somebody with a basic knowledge of astronomical concepts, should enjoy reading this book for fun as well. It might even inspire an astronomer with new directions for further research into exoplanets, as some unanswered questions are proposed.

On Clinton's Quid Pro Quo Sexual Harassment and Other Salacious Intrigues

Russell L. Riley. *Inside the Clinton White House: An Oral History.* $21.95. 442pp, 6X9", ISBN: 978-0-19-088849-7. Oxford: Oxford University Press, 2018.

***

An exhaustive review of materials on the Clinton White House, based on 400 hours of interviews with over sixty people, including British Prime Minister Tony Blair. The story begins with Clinton's first presidential run until the end of the presidency. The first part is about how the campaign came together, but then the book is organized by subjects rather than chronologically, with reviews of his domestic and economic policy, foreign policy, and review of each of the members of Clinton's team. The Preface points out that Clinton's political career's last act was Hillary's loss in the 2016 campaign (a run that he was heavily involved in). It also explains that this soft cover edition of the book only adds two new interviewees, Blair and Elaine Kamarck. The interviews were conducted across a decade at the University of Virginia in a "nonpartisan research institute". The author, Russell L. Riley, assisted with collecting some additional interviews in the field. The book is based on the publicly accessible (since November 2014) interviews on the Miller Center's website.

The book is logically organized to allow readers to follow the natu-
rally digressive interviews. Each section begins with a summary of a
portion of Clinton's political life, followed by the name of the inter-
viewee, their relationship to the president, and a quote on their take
of this part of history. Each interviewee is allotted anywhere from a
paragraph to a few pages to give their thoughts. They were probably all
asked the same set of questions on the topics these headings are about,
resulting in these categorized replies. On the other hand, this book
seems to transcribe most of the relevant replies rather than picking only
those which convey new information. For example, the first comment
is from Susan Thomases, a political activist, who begins by explaining
that Clinton "knew it was hard" to attempt running for office "and he
might not make it, but that was his objective…" (4). This is a very cli-
ché comment; Thomases is described as Bill's "friend", so it is only nat-
ural that she would want to talk about him in a friendly way, but these
types of surface summaries suggest that she does not want to name any
details perhaps to cover up something that cannot be put into public
record. If you were describing a fellow politician's first run, would you
bother pondering on the likelihood it was going to be "hard"? Then,
David Kusnet, a White House speechwriter, discusses that Clinton is
a Southern Baptist from a small town. Then, he jumps at random to
various causes Clinton supported aside from religion. Somebody who
is reading this book casually for enjoyment would have a difficult time
finding a unifying plotline and would lose interest. Perhaps, one can
skip around to read what famous people like Madeleine Albright said,
but her first comment appears only on page 30, and she gives the short-
est response up to that point: "Getting to Little Rock from Washington
is like going to outer space." This is a response to a chapter on "Staff-
ing the Campaign." The replies also make for difficult reading because
most of them appear without a question before them, just as com-
ments on the topic of the chapter. Occasionally, a question is inserted,
when asking for additional information, as in, "Were you concerned
from your perch about the personal issues with Clinton?" This ques-
tion seems a strange one, since it's unclear what personal issues, might
be meant, but the interviewee, Elaine Kamarck, a DLC strategist, ex-
plains in her response that they knew of "some of the women he had
had affairs with, and we knew he had had many affairs. Al talked to Bill
and got assurances that all of that was in the past." Curiously, she goes
on to explain that she was not concerned about these women because

"these were all women who had a stake in his success" (22). This is a description of quid pro quo sexual harassment, wherein women obtain something related to their careers in exchange for sex. If this is a random specific detail out of the book, it seems that when interviewees are giving cliché or vague descriptions, they are avoiding saying something this blunt. Perhaps if the interviewees asked more follow up questions like this one, they would have obtained more incriminating details. Though, I'm sure plenty of dirt is already scattered across this book. Journalists can probably find many salacious headlines in this book. Of course, since the Preface begins by saying that Clinton's political career is now officially over, it's too late for such headlines to make a political difference, and therefore the dirt is now in the realm of history rather than journalism.

Answers to Popular Nutrition Questions

P. K. Newby. *Food & Nutrition: What Everyone Needs to Know.* $16.95. 294pp, 6X9". ISBN: 978-0-19-084663-3. Oxford: Oxford University Press, 2018.

***

I had to request this title for review as it promised to answer all of the questions I have been searching for answers to on the web and in YouTube videos since I went on a vegan diet a year and a half ago. In it a nutritional scientist answers 134 questions on how to attain a "health-giving diet". It is especially concerned with creating a "sustainable" diet that is good for the planet rather than solely one that improves individual health. P. K. Newby is an Associate Professor at Harvard, so her advice should be more reliable than your typical vegan guru's. To be honest, my current interests are in my own health, with the planet coming in second. The book begins with a chapter on "Nutrition Issues", which explains contemporary diets, the ruling food companies and the impact of food on the environment. On the surface, this looked like guru-territory on first glance, but the details in the chapter are diving into details I have not come across in my casual reading. For example, the subsection on "traditional and contemporary diets" begins by defining what "traditional" means in this context, before jumping into major food categories like "cereal grasses", a topic which is closely digested as containing some of the first-cultivated major crops. Each cereal, like rice is defined in terms of its territory, climate, and energy consumed in its production. Any YouTube video maker can really find a lot of details here to recycle. So many discussions touch on traditional diets as being healthier alternatives for humans than processed foods, but few other works I looked at define this closely exactly what traditional diets around the world consist of. The section on who runs the food system also surprises with statistics on the large percentage of population that work in agriculture in the developing world compared with only 1% in the US and UK. The chapter ends with a paragraph that brushes on four (near)famines in 2017 that affected millions in South Sudan, Somalia, Nigeria, and Yemen. Basically, every paragraph in this book is full of statistics, facts, nutritional research and other useful or interesting information. I find myself drawn into this story, and my own nutritional concerns fade as I keep reading this study. If somebody is purely interested in their own health, though, they probably would have a difficult time finding the needed data in this book. On the other hand, each of these topics really needs a lot more attention. For example, there is a brief section called "What are the causes of food poisoning, and how can it be reduced?" There are four pieces of advice in bold towards the end of the three pages allotted to the topic (wash hands, separate raw food, cook to kill, chill food). The section describes the various types of common food borne illnesses, but then offers this basic advice to avoid it. The facts suggest that one can catch these diseases by going to just about any restaurant even in wealthy countries, or by eating from a cruise ship buffet, or by eating raw vegetables from the local supermarket. Well, I already knew most of that. I would really appreciate a more practical guide for avoiding this problem. Surely, there are ways of telling if food is affected, or more advice that could be gained. How does food need to be cooked more precisely? How can I check raw vegetables to make sure they're safe to it? The author's motivations are also hazy. In a section on "processed" food, she sides with food processing in contrast with most nutritionists I've been reading who argue that processing food and adding sugar, salt and chemicals to it is a major cause of health problems. Instead of going in this direction, Newby sites a study that found that there is "little difference in healthfulness on average comparing nutrient intake... across a broad range of processed food levels" (57). I am recalling watching a documentary that mentioned that some top nutrition scholars are paid by the food industry for promoting their foods as healthy, and this siding with food processing suggests that Newby has fallen prey to this problem. In the section on "red and processed meats" relationship with cancer, she offers a more conventional summary that this link has been verified by studies, but does color it with rosier colors, saying that some processed and red meat consumption should be a part of a healthy diet (60-1). Throughout, Newby attempts to criticize the gurus' bogus nutritional advice. It is easy to slip into obsession when following a vegan or otherwise restricting diet, so that one probably doesn't realize that the rules he or she is following are potentially not grounded in reality. Newby does a good job explaining scientific findings on each of these trends; for example, avoiding pasteurization of milk is explained as a major health hazard confirmed by dozens of scientific studies. Some of the explanations are only brushing on the surface. For example, I really wanted to learn more about vitamin D, so I read this section, hoping to find if a brief trip outside or keeping my windows open would generate some vitamin D, or if eating less than the recommended value daily (but still a decent amount from margarine) might be sufficient, or if I definitely need a supplement. Instead of answering any of this, the section simply defined vitamin D and explained that its lack causes disease.

In summary, anybody who is going on an extreme diet of any sort should read this book or a book like it to understand the basics of nutritional science. I plan on reading it more closely at leisure later on to mine it for some useful details I might be missing.

A Pop History of Africa's Golden Age

Francois-Xavier Fauvelle. *The Golden Rhinoceros*. $29.95. 280pp, 5.5X8.5", 18 images. ISBN: 978-0-691181264. Princeton: Princeton University Press, November 13, 2018.

***

The history of Africa is particularly relevant today because the discussion on the origins of humanity has been popping up in everything from racist rhetoric in the presidential campaign, to Black Lives Matter, to new research that suggests that European humans have more of the Neanderthal in them. Thus, this history of medieval Africa in its Golden Age should answer a lot of these questions on the side of African pride and power. Francois-Xavier Fauvelle picks up the story at the birth of Islam in the seventh century, and carries it to the first explorations of this continent by Europeans. On top of archival research, Fauvelle relies on his own archaeological research. He reconstructs this distant past without a sufficient written record by describing and interpreting its art, maps, as well as the precious accounts left by geographers and travelers. The book looks at the multiple dimensions of life in Africa, including trade, religion, politics, art, and personal lives. The titles of the chapters are pretty cryptic, inviting readers to read them in full rather than skimming to find just the parts of particular interest; for example, one title is, "In the Belly of the Sperm Whale." Most of the chapters do include some specification regarding the region of Africa covered as well as the centuries discussed, with most in a chronological order, though some focus on a single city like Ghana across the bulk of its history. Some chapters look at a single ruler such as the King of Zafun. All of these chapters seem to be structured around a coherent, engaging narrative with a beginning, middle and end, or in other words, they attempt to catch the reader's attention with an engaging story rather than reviewing the details of the history for its own sake.

Each chapter includes a black and white illustration of the central concept, such as a piece of architecture, or a whale. Given the focus on art, it's surprising that there are no archival photos of the art and architecture discussed. Given the condensed bibliographical notes, and the conversational writing style and illustrations, this book seems to be written for a younger audience, perhaps high school or introductory college history classes. For example, Chapter 1 includes this opening sentence: "One of the excerpts tells us about a certain land, Molin, where the people are black…" (17). This refers to the contents of a book, *Jingxingji*, described in the previous paragraph from Guangzhoe, China in 762. This introduction is suitable for younger readers, but a researcher in this field would probably find it to be too simplistic. Later on, the author asks if "we are forced to accept a 652 date for the signing…" (34). A conventional historian typically does not discuss unknown historical dates in these terms. Why would anybody be forced to accept an unknown?

In summary, this book is too chatty and non-specific for my taste.

I prefer purely informative history that delivers the facts. But, if somebody is looking for lighter reading and is interested in the intriguing topics it promises to deliver, they should be happy with the contents herein.

Out-of-Context Snippets from Soldiers at War

Marian Eide & Michael Gibler. *After Combat: True War Stories from Iraq and Afghanistan*. $29.95. 256pp, 6X9". ISBN: 978-1-64012-023-5. Lincoln: Potomac Books: Nebraska University Press, 2018.

***

A collection of combat accounts from some of the 2.5 million soldiers U.S. has deployed to Iraq and Afghanistan as part of the War on Terror. Not all of these soldiers held weapons or shot somebody, but all were affected by listening to mortars at night, or otherwise being fully engaged in a warzone. These soldiers come from all branches of the military (marines, air force), with experience ranges from new entrants to retirees. It is a bit troubling that they are speaking anonymously, as it would be difficult to verify their stories to check for accuracy. I can understand how soldiers who are still active probably would not speak as frankly if their real names were used, but I have read other books where names are used for soldiers that took part in historic combat. If I was telling my war story, I would want my name to by in the by-line so I might use it as a publication credit in my CV. The soldiers in this book are touching on sanctions, and other failures, so I guess those bits would not be CV-worthy. One of the authors is a Texas history professor and the other, Gibler, served as an infantry officer for twenty-eight years, so they should have a good balance of understanding both the historical and the military components of this content. This book has a very similar structure to the Clinton interviews book I covered earlier in this set of reviews. The chapters are broken down into the twenty broad questions these soldiers were asked: enlisting, missions, explosions, low points, close calls, combat, comrades, chain of command, killing people, enemies, and topics related to grief, loss and other emotions. Each chapter begins with a brief paragraph summary of the topics raised in the chapter; perhaps these summaries are extended versions of the questions the interviewees were asked. These are followed by paragraphs of varied length from each interviewee separated by section breaks. There are no explanations regarding the rank, status and the like of who the storyteller is unless they include these details in their descriptions. While in theory there are a lot of curious details in this collection, in reality, a lot of things could have been taken out as repetitions, clichés or general and uninteresting information. For example, one of these answers begins with, "The cultural shock in and of itself was huge. I went from an over-abundance of things: a home, a place to sleep that's guaranteed. Yeah, there are threats here, but not like over there…" (77). Without context, this is very ominous: what threats exist here? Obviously, this is just a soldier who's just chatting about his impression of culture shock, but what kind of a reader would benefit from reading something like this? Another soldier talks about the "thrill" of warfare, admitting that he's done "cocaine" before but that it surpasses it, especially when he was "driving past the Iraqi tomb of the unknown", which made him feel particularly alive (150). Somebody's tomb made him feel energized? Or this one: "there were a lot of ethical issues that surfaced". This paragraph later explains that one of these issues was potentially treating and discharging a person only for them to possibly be "shot in a Sunni hospital (if they're Shia)" (220). Why would a treated patient need to return to another hospital, and why would they be shot there? It's extremely disorienting reading bits of history and biography without adequate annotations and explanations. For a researcher, if someone manages to dig through all this and finds the bits where war crimes, violence against innocent people and the like is covered, these bits cannot really be quoted in a coherent way in future research. Every paragraph is already taken out of context, so contextualizing it as any scholarly study has to do would be impossible. Thus, the book seems to be intended for the soldiers who went through the wars and want to read how other soldiers perceived the experience. I would recommend writing a version of this book that cuts out most of the irrelevant information, and offers primarily historical and strategic descriptions with interviews being used only as supporting evidence in proper context.

Digressions on the Biases of Scientific Naming

Michael Ohl; Translated by Elisabeth Lauffer. *The Art of Naming.* 294pp, 6X9". ISBN: 978-0-262-03776-1. Cambridge: MIT Press, 2018.

****

All writers have contemplated the act of naming. Should a name be symbolic? Should it be phonetically or aesthetically pleasing? What are the rules for naming species that might help a writer name a fictional alien or fantastical species? This book attempts to address this naming art in a single thorough study. Since there are 1.8 million named species, there is plenty of ground for research in this field. The cover explains that the rules for scientific naming "in standard nomenclature, the generic name followed by specific name—go back to Linnaeus; but they are open to idiosyncrasy and individual expression." The cover of this book is beautifully and elegantly designed with several named with tags species of winged insects against a sterile white background. Several curious archival photographs from various uniquely named species illustrate the book, as well as photos of the scientists who named some of these species. Most of these images were taken by the author at the exhibits and collections of the Museum fur Naturkunde in Berlin.

The first chapter's name attracts attention, "1 Hitler and the Fledermaus", and it delivers on the promise to shock: on March 3, 1942, the Berliner Morgenpost newspaper attempted to announce that the German Society for Mammalogy passed a resolution to change the names for shrew "spitzmaus" to "spitzer" and the name for bat "Fledermaus" to "fleder" because the original names were misleading. The newspaper then received a threatening letter from Martin Bormann, Adolf Hitler's private secretary that stated that they will be sent to "the construction battalion on the Russian front" if they did not immediately retract the renaming, and the paper immediately complied, so that these names remain to this day in their confusing original form. This is a great example of how names can become hotly debated political tools. It definitely draws readers into the book.

While this book is saturated with stories about how things are named and naming controversies, it is a bit frustrating for a researcher who might be interested in finding practical information on how to name a character or a new species to search for specifically relevant guidance. The second chapter begins with Armand David's journey into naming plants, then has a section on if a panda is a bear, with later sections on nomenclature, and validity. Basically, most of the chapter discusses how irregular naming has been, wherein random institutions or individuals who discover species or influence those who discover them have chosen names somewhat arbitrarily rather than in a systematic, scientific way. A section called "Naming Rights for Sale" really stresses this. In the *Chasing New Horizons* book that I reviewed earlier in this set, there is a discussion on how Pluto was named after the wife of the donor that sponsored the observatory that found the semi-planet.

If a scientist buys this book in the hope of finding concrete guidance on how to name a new species, he or she has discovered, it is unlikely he or she will walk away with a clear sense on how to proceed beyond the basics. But they might realize that they are supposed to name the species after their funders or give it a political name that might inspire future funding of their work. This is a great read for those interested in history, archeology, biology, and naming. It is written for general readers who might want to escape with a good book but dislike fiction, preferring true dramatic stories.

A Precious Collection of Genre-Setting Gothic Tales from Doyle

Arthur Conan Doyle. *Gothic Tales*. Oxford World's Classics. $14.95. 550pp, 6X9". ISBN: 978-0-19-873430-7. Oxford: Oxford University Press, 2018.

****

Whenever I feel a bit of strain for inspiration as I attempt to write one of my fictional projects, I typically open a random page in a collection of Edgar Allen Poe's short stories. And when I am searching for the best way to structure a mystery, I tend to return to Conan Doyle's Sherlock Holmes and Agatha Christie. Why have these early stories captured readers' imaginations? Somehow, they seem to be better than recent best-selling or highly literary mysteries. What sets them apart? It is not their density of description, but rather something about their easy flow and inviting manner that brings readers into the tricks the authors set for their villains and heroes. So, naturally, when I saw the option to request Arthur Conan Doyle's *Gothic Tales*, I jumped on it. In my scholarly research into the mystery genre, I read about the other genre fictions that Doyle practiced, but I have not read any of them in full. So, it is with great interest that I open these pages.

All of these stories originally appeared in magazines, and most of them in the *Strand*. One of the things that puzzled me about Doyle when I researched him was his spiritualism, or the support of mystics and other quacks who argued for the existence of the supernatural. It is possible that Doyle propagated for these causes in order to lift sales of his Gothic short stories, or perhaps his true spiritual beliefs are expressed in these works. The "Introduction" does a great job discussing this link as well as explaining that Doyle might have been interested in spiritualism and psychology because of his father's history of alcoholism and insanity. Another macabre element of Doyle's life was his work as a military medic, wherein he dealt with an outbreak of enteric fever that "cost 5,000 lives" (xvi). It further explains that Doyle wrote an imperialist history of this war shortly thereafter, *The Great Boer War* (1900), which makes excuses for British concentration camps.

The "Introduction" concludes by arguing that Doyle became more anxious in his later Gothic tales about the "modern world": "In 'How It Happened' (1913), a motorist loses control of his car and hurtles downhill to his death. In 'The Horror of the Heights' (1913), an aviator discovers a hostile new ecosystem high in the stratosphere. In 'The Nightmare Room' (1921), a disturbing domestic scenario is gradually revealed in all its horror as a film set. In 'The Lift' (1922), a group of tourists find themselves suspended in an elevator high above the ground, at the mercy of a homicidal religious maniac" (xxxiii). This is a great summary of the types of unique plots covered in these stories. Each one is unlike the hyper-formulaic horror films popular today. If these stories are more popularly read by producers and script writers, they might borrow some of these new concepts that have not been as exploited as Doyle's Holmes stories have been.

The first tale in the collection, "The American's Tale", includes a great deal of linguistic complexity, as Jefferson Adams relates his convoluted and chopped-up story in a strange variant of the American accent. The second story, "The Captain of the 'Polestar'", is an incredibly dense account of a medical student. Everything from the geology of

Amsterdam Island, to the crew of the ship, to the narrator's relationship with the captain is minutely described. Since Doyle worked in a similar medical role on ships shortly after graduating from medical school, these read like a fictionalized version of his own journals. Later stories are a bit lighter on description, focusing more on actions and dialogue. For example, the third story, "The Winning Shot", begins with a description of a dangerous man the public has been warned to look out for, building tension through this danger at the start, and then building on it across adventures like a rifle competition. Density returns in some of the later stories as well as the setting of dangerous sea voyages in stories like "J. Habakuk Jephson's Statement." The complexity of the linguistics and structures of these stories hide some of the common tropes of horror, but they are still very much a presence in the works, as, for example, "The Surgeon of Gaster Fell" begins with the trope of howling wind: "Bleak and wind-swept is the little town of Kirkby-Malhouse, harsh and forbidding are the fells upon which it stands" (167). The narrators and characters express a constant sense of dread common to horror, but also slip into "a dash of romance", as for example, the narrator in "'De Profundis'" begins the story: "For the soul is swayed by the waters, as the waters are by the moon, and when the great highways of an empire are along such roads as these, so full of strange sights and sounds, with danger ever running alike a hedge on either side of the course, it is a dull mind indeed which does not bear away with it some trace of such a passage" (201).

This is definitely not light reading, but it is a great source of detail on the period described. It also offers intriguing and innovative approaches to the horror genre on every page. The stories travel in surprising pathways and mesmerize readers with amazing sights and adventures. All researchers into Doyle should study this collection closely. It is also required reading for graduate students and established researchers alike of the Gothic tale. Poe's tales are more readable or approachable as their digressions are wrapped into more condensed and direct dramas. But by wondering away on many curious tangents Doyle shows a greater range this genre is capable of.

Practical Guide to Copyright Law

Neil Weinstock Netanel. *Copyright: What Everyone Needs to Know.*

$16.95. 228pp. ISBN: 978-0-19-994116-2. Oxford: Oxford University Press, 2018.

****

This is a practical guide to copyright law. It does not introduce any new research, but rather restates the facts in a comprehensive way. I definitely had to request this title because I have frequently googled specific copyright laws as I have been running my publishing company. Questions frequently come up regarding reprints, quotes in fair use, and various other potential infringements by others or by the authors I publish or by these authors of their own work. So, this book should help me find more precise answers to all of these questions when I need them next. Online sources typically only skim the surface and it is difficult to verify or trust most of them. In contrast, this book is written by the Chair in Law at the University of California at Los Angeles School of Law, Neil Weinstock Netanel, so his answers are definitive. Of course, this information is not only relevant for publishers nowadays, but to everyday web users, as the cover explains. Anybody can share something that is protected by copyrights on their social media or cloud storage account, stumbling into a potential lawsuit without realizing they are breaking the law. I have stumbled into websites that are offering ebooks of titles I have released for free perhaps to bait potential buyers into uploading a virus or perhaps to garner traffic to their website, without permission from me or from the author. Since I offer electronic review copies for free, it is likely users of review sites use them to steal content. It seems likely that they might also be selling content they are stealing under other names for a profit. These types of thefts are incredibly prevalent, and somebody purchasing a book online is unlikely to know they are breaking the law with each such purchase. Theft of original works have probably led to some of the consolidation and bankruptcies within the publishing industry, so these thefts are hardly innocuous to small publishers who gamble a significant part of their net worth with every new risky release. I love free and cheap books as much as anybody. I received dozens of free books for this set of reviews. I also thoroughly enjoy using free Google Books or free Amazon LookInside options as part of my research because my local library does not offer Interlibrary Loan or other methods of requesting the rare books I typically need. I have also narrowed my media watching to Netflix and YouTube to avoid paying fees for cable or movie theaters. So, I can understand critics who argue for more accessibility to the world of media, but if the price of books, films and the rest drops down to zero, only creators who are non-profits or doing the work for fun rather than a career will be left to create content. So, those who work on the margins of this dilemma, like music producers, definitely should be familiar with the law so that they sample and remix work in a way that is legal and fair to the original creators.

A world without original art, and instead crowded by stolen reproductions is a very grim and desolate world indeed.

On Clay's Adventures in the Turbulent Politics

James C. Klotter. *Henry Clay: The Man Who Would Be President.* $34.95. 510pp, 6X9". ISBN: 978-0-19-049804-7. Oxford: Oxford University Press, 2018.

****

A history of Henry Clay's political career and the events that surrounded it, rather than a biography of Clay's life. The main political struggles described are those around Clay's two unsuccessful presidential runs that took place between 1824 and 1848. Clay ran the Whig Party for some of this stretch, but still could not win its nomination, as on at least one of these occasions the Whig candidate did succeed in winning the presidency. Clay is portrayed as a conciliator who brought about the Missouri Compromise and the Compromise of 1850, as well as many other compromises that kept the United States as a unified whole. The book is heavy on notes and research and is illustrated with some telling cartoons, drawings and photographs. Clay had political roots in Kentucky, so it is only natural that the author, James C. Klotter, a professor of History at Georgetown College a past executive director of the Kentucky Historical Society, spent a good deal of time in the Kentucky Historical Society's Clay archive when researching this book. The "Preface" begins with a note about the 1861 monument dedication in Kentucky in Henry Clay's honor, with a note that he was "their state's most famous political leader, a man who had tried to avoid the war [Civil War] now raging around them" (xiii). Clay was born in

Virginia, but made Kentucky his adopted political base residence. The primary question Klotter set out to answer with this study is: "Why did Clay not win the presidency?" (xvi) Clearly, this heavy book was needed to simply begin answering this question. This is a great time for such questions as President Trump has managed to win this job once, and despite numerous accusations against him for anything from theft to treason, he might go on to win a second term. Is there an inherent corruption in the American political system that keeps the most fit (best educated, most talented, most brilliant strategists) out of the top office? Anybody who is considering running for office in the United States needs to read books like this one to begin to understand what drives American voting habits and what about the primaries process might be screening out the best fit in favor of the most corrupted. On the other hand, Clay was born in obscurity and had a limited education (facts that he stressed to improve his public image), and he did a lot of winning in politics to get to the top of the Whig party, including becoming a US representative, US senator, diplomat, and secretary of state. Klotter contradicts some of the myth Clay reinforced, arguing that Clay's father was not an impoverished minister, but rather came "from a distinguished family that had been in Virginia almost from the first English settlement" (2).

Overall, this is a brilliantly executed history of a period and a presidential hopeful. Every page is rich with revelations and surprises and offers lessons for current politicians and historians alike. A graduate or undergraduate class can be taught with this book alone. The research is immaculate and touches every conceivable stone available. The stories related at every turn include adventures like Aaron Burr's arrival in Kentucky after he was disgraced for killing Alexander Hamilton in a duel (214) to the gifts Clay received after his 1844 defeat, which included silver pitchers (of all things) (328). This book, in many ways, makes for more exciting reading than top formulaic mysteries.

The Comprehensive History of European Law from Its Origins to the Near-Present

Antonio Padoa-Schioppa. *A History of Law in Europe: From the Early Middle Ages to the Twentieth Century.* 808pp, 6X9". ISBN: 978-1-107-18069-7. Cambridge: Cambridge University Press, 2018.

****

I requested this title because I occasionally write non-fiction and fiction that touches on the past, and frequently I find it necessary to look up laws from different periods to avoid making incorrect assumptions. Laws change yearly and certainly have mutated over the centuries. And laws vary widely between different countries. So, this is a very helpful attempt to summarize the history of law in Europe across the Middle Ages and through the Twentieth Century, an amazing range of places and times to squeeze into a single (though heavy) volume. Modern laws frequently seem barely comprehensible. Why does America still have a death penalty? Why are the debate about the legalization of pot or abortion still raging on in the modern age? This history attempts to look back to Roman and Christian laws to explain how they mutated into what we are familiar with today. Anybody who complains about the current legal system should benefit from the lessons from the past herein. This is a first translation of this copious work into English. It is authored by Antonio Padoa-Schioppa, Professor Emeritus and former Dean of the Law School at the University of Milan. The book is chronologically organized, with the first part covering everything from the fifth to the eleventh centuries, and the last one on the twentieth century. Rather than being organized by country, within each part, different chapters address major changes and trends. For example, a chapter focuses on "Christianity, Church and Law" while another looks at the "University: Students and Teachers." Each chapter title is intriguing and offers insights into the types of things we have come to take for granted; for example, a chapter on "Legal Professions" looks into the origins of various different legal sub-categories, such as notaries, colleges of judges and advocates, and justices. Another chapter examines the various "Sources of Law" for individual countries (Italy, France, Germany and others), examining the influences on the law made by their individual "state legislation, local customs, city and guild statutes, feudal law, Roman *ius commune*, canon law and the decisions of the superior courts" (368). The discussion veers into politics as motivation for unique trends in the law, such as the origins of the Austrian criminal codes in Napoleonic codes and the research conducted by "illustrious Viennese professors and jurists" who drafted Austrian texts.

In summary, researchers and writers who touch on Europe across its history can benefit from having this thorough review in their library. It answers many of the questions that modern legal scholars might take for granted. We have retained the inheritance of these ancient legal precedents, so we have to understand what motivated their original creation. Only by understanding the biases, preferences, and the like of their founders can be pick the laws that are still morally or logically suitable and which ones should fade into the history books instead of continuing as legal facts.

More Nonsense About Linguistics

John Bowers. *Deriving Syntactic Relations: Cambridge Studies in Linguistics: 151.* 296pp. ISBN: 978-1-107-09675-2. Cambridge: Cambridge University Press, 2018.

*

Linguistics is a field of study that is undeniably necessary in our present times. Why? Every professor and high school teacher knows the answer. The volume of plagiarized essays is overwhelming. The essay mills are producing countless nonsensical and repetitive essays and selling them for a few dollars. Students are stealing information from Wikipedia and plastering it into their "creations". Aside from this momentous problem, the volume of copyright lawsuits that accuses writers, musicians and others of theft of original content is climbing. There is a dire need for coherent linguistic analysis in courtrooms and classrooms. Instead of taking on these practical problems, most popular or established linguists engage in the practice of nonsense linguistics. It is easy to spot contributions to this field because they inevitably quote as their inspiration Chomsky or Lacan. The second most telling element is repetition of the same nonsensical phrases or even sentences with slight variations, as if the author is practicing self-plagiarism for the sake of proving that if readers cannot comprehend nonsense, they will assume the work is brilliant simply to avoid reading it. The repetitions in this text begin on its cover. The front inside flap replicates the book summary paragraphs from the back cover. Just imagine a book with two identical copies of the author's biography on different parts of the cover, or what if two of these biographies were repeated one after the other on the back cover alone... The author is likely to have won a contract to publish this convoluted title because he is a professor in the Department of Linguistics at Cornell University. This is his third book in this field; one of these earlier studies was *Arguments as Relations*, and its title alone implies that it is also cyclical and nonsensical. What do you think is the logical relationship between arguments and relations in general? Relationship between relations? Arguments about relatives? Arguments that relate different things to each other? If this contemplation about the meaning of the title is nonsensical, imagine what an analysis of a few sentences might be like... Funny enough, the first sentence of the "Introduction" touches on this "concept" of "relations": "There have been a number of attempts in modern era to argue that the primitives of syntactic theory should be relations (or dependencies) between words rather than constituents" (1). Then he jumps into naming a dozen random past nonsensical studies from this field, as if these notes are going to explain the lack of meaning in the opening sentence. What possible part of human language can exclude words? Constituents, regardless as to what this term means, are words themselves. If every part of language is a word, how can anything be outside of this term and yet an element used to express written language? This type of a self-contradicting opening sentence works to keep readers from attempting to find fault with the argument. If nobody can interpret the meaning within an inherent self-contradiction, then it is incredibly difficult to prove that it is nonsensical with help from logic. If I began this review thus, "The beginning interpret meaning element goes to exclude naming in syntactic theory and professor studies words"; how would you begin criticizing this string of random words put together in a nonsensical pattern? Why would you want to spend hours attempting to decode such nonsense? The only difference between pure nonsense composed of completely randomly selected words from a dictionary and linguistic research nonsense is that the latter tends to repeat the same strings of nonsense, referring to earlier studies that also said the same nonsense as proof that the research has been verified by established researchers. In addition, this particular study uses diagrams and convoluted theories that attempt to appear like serious linguistic research. Many sections begin with no introductory sentence other than "Let's consider next the following two orders: (11) a. Dem N Num A (=Cinque's (6c))..." Then, he goes on to explain the relations between the different categories summarized, touching on their common roots.

This particular section ends in the middle of a thought without coming to any conclusions, with the promise that this "is a question I return to in §4.1.8" (134-5). If any scholar is seriously attempting to explain any concept, he or she has to begin a thought by summarizing the concept, then offer an explanation and in the end summarize what the research means to digest it for the reader. In contrast, linguistic nonsense research begins in the middle of a random thought, introduces nonsensical or extremely convoluted research, and then moves on to other topics without explaining the relationship between the random words just presented. When will publishers begin rejecting nonsense, sparing researchers like myself valuable time, and allowing for the publication of truly useful linguistic studies?

A String of Convoluted Definitions on English from Its Birth

Olga Fischer, Hendrik de Smet and Wim Van der Wurff. *A Brief History of English Syntax*. 240pp, 6X9". ISBN: 978-0-521-74797-4. Cambridge: Cambridge University Press, 2018.

***

My hope for this book was that it would be a clear and concise history of English syntax, as the title promises. The introduction and the back cover also promise this helpful textbook, but the interior delivers a very convoluted and jumbled set of ideas. Of course, delivering the history of all of English's syntax is an extremely tall order. English has warped on numerous dimensions from its roots that lacked clear grammatical or spelling rules, which opted for regional, class and other variations. Attempting to read a text in English from 1,500 years ago is definitely a journey into an entirely foreign language with entirely different rules of syntax. As the introduction explains, English has been impacted by German, Viking, Norman, Celtic as well as numerous other languages and their rules. This book attempts to summarizes the changes into categories, such as the "rapid loss of inflexions" through contact with other linguistic populations. This might be a doomed quest because the nature of language mutation was not led by unified movements but rather by individuals in isolated regions making sudden changes across most of this 1,500-year history. Only relatively recently did dictionaries and grammar books unify the language and allow for kings or academics to control linguistic change. Can there be clearly identifiable changes in "word order, the noun phrase and verb phrase, changing relations between clausal constituents and the development of new subordinate constructions" that can be summarized in a short study? As a researcher in the field of linguistics, I certainly hope that patterns can be identified and explained, as they can help to interpret older texts, and evaluate the age of texts based on their syntax. The introduction ends with "Table 1.1 Overview of syntactic categories and their changes", which attempts to summarize the major shifts across Old English, Middle English and Modern English with a focus on case form and function, determiners, quantifiers, adjectives, the aspect-system, the tense system, the mood system, the voice system, subjects, objects, adverbs and the like. For one of these, the voice-system, the authors examine how indirect passive was absent in the earliest period, developed in the middle period and became fully present in Modern English. The table shows which chapters touch on this particular subject: "7.5 Passive Constructions: Gains and Losses". This section begins by referring the reader to two other chapters for additional explanations of these constructions (6 and 9) instead of summarizing what this construction is. Then, a brief definition is given: "changes in the realization of the arguments of the passive verb in a finite clause", followed by a set of examples that compares direct, indict and prepositional passive voice (148-9). Several notes interrupt this very complex discussion by referring to research conducted into these topics by others. The story is also interrupted by contradictions in the linguistic evidence, such as the problem that "dative fronted passives had died out before the new indirect passives arrived", thus, making it impossible that this previously proposed conclusion could be correct. Later in the section, examples include the very difficult to comprehend (for a modern reader) Old English examples. The conclusion to this section focuses on fine points that are impossible for anybody but an advanced grammarian to grasp in a paragraph-long single sentence with extremely complex grammar. In other words, just to read this single sentence, somebody needs to be an advanced grammarian, and then he or she needs to know the definitions of the numerous terms involved like "experiencer" and "(medio)-passive" (definitions which are not offered clearly in a way that would allow for comprehension) to begin to comprehend the meaning. Having taken PhD-level grammar courses, I can report that the difficult level of this book is far beyond the most difficult grad textbook I navigated through. It would take a year for anybody to simply read this book as he or she slowly looks up each of the barely explained terms and works through the examples (including translating the parts that are in Old English). If you are a linguistic historian who has written a couple of books on Old and Middle English, you should eventually understand this book (at which point you might be able to prove that its conclusions have inaccuracies in them). If you do not fall into this category, do not attempt to read this book; it would be a futile effort.

Great Promises and Rambling Delivery of a Linguistic Soup

Ian Roberts. *The Wonders of Language or How to Make Noises and Influence People*. 230pp. ISBN: 978-1-316-60441-0. Cambridge: Cambridge University Press, 2018.

***

After the last few linguistic titles, I am a bit hesitant to dive into this one. But the playful red lopsided "Noises" in the cover design suggests that this book is created with the general public in mind, so hopefully it is digestible. The back cover's promise is ambitious, proposing an "accessible introduction to the main discoveries and theories about language" with a look at the various branches of this field, "phonetics, phonology, morphology, syntax, semantics and pragmatics, as well as historical linguistics, sociolinguistics and psycholinguistics." Since these are pretty much all of the fields under the broad umbrella of language study and the book is only a couple hundred pages long, this seems like a tall order. The author's experience is also promising, as Ian is teaching at the University of Cambridge, and has published eight scholarly books. The chapters of the book are divided under the broad categories of linguistics named above. The last chapter makes a curious promise: "How to Build a Language: Language Typology and Universals." This is particularly interesting for me because I'm currently pondering how language is created for my first science fiction novel. Would aliens have an entirely different type of language? Can they be using visuals, sounds, or other forms of communication that would not be translatable into English? Or is there something innate about language that would not change even across light years of space? Ian asks similar questions in this chapter's opening paragraph, but he digresses much further without offering answers. He goes on to name previous research that looked at patterns in the main elements of language across dozens of different languages across the world. The order of subject and object varies, as do many of the other rules that are consistent in English alone. Meanwhile, the basic elements of language are found in all of the world's languages. Then, he dives into a discussion that some orders are more common in sentences than others. Then, he attempts to explain this through psycholinguistics, but does not really get to a solution. Chomsky is named later in this chapter, so one can guess that not much sense appears, and it's only natural that the concluding paragraph is: "What their answers are we just don't know, but we're working on it" (180). I'm saddened to report that my hopes for this book have fallen through. Instead of explaining linguistics in a way that students can grasp and digest, this book is a conversational exercise in speculation that offers some clear definitions and examples, but fails to be concise or clear. The main problem is that instead of defining what each of the covered fields is and offering explanations of their main concepts, the author babbles about narrow topics within these fields, giving a review of a few studies. This shows a lack of the broad knowledge necessary to write a textbook that encompasses such an enormous field. Perhaps a dozen books later, Ian will arrive at this comprehension and his twentieth book will finally manage to offer a digested linguistic meal.

Should the U.S. Stop Propagandizing on the Inferiority of Latin America?

Lars Schoultz. *In Their Own Best Interest: A History of the U.S. Effort to Improve Latin Americans.* 392pp, 6X9". ISBN: 978-0-674-98414-1. Cambridge: Harvard University Press, 2018.

****

It is always enjoyable to read research that departs from the formula common to a topic. In this case, most of the books on Latin America and U.S. relations I previously read attempt to interpret the paternalistic relationship in a positive way, searching for new ways to help out southern neighbors. Unlike them, this book questions this relationship and the wisdom of U.S. dictating proper government or oral hygiene methods to Latin America. U.S. barely has a rudimentary understanding or execution of democratic principles itself if the last few elections are any indication. The electoral college has overruled the popular vote in two recent elections, and the extremely close votes suggest that there is broad election fraud. People are less likely to vote in tight elections, and they are less likely to vote if they believe polls have already chosen a winner. And America's two-party system prevents candidates with innovative ideologies or those who have not been corrupted by the paid-to-play politics these two parties promote from being able to compete fairly. What about this destructive and anti-representative system is worth spreading to other countries? Lars Schoultz explains how the current paternalistic role for the U.S. came about, dating it back to the Progressive Era. The duality of the Cold War built the concept in American minds that communism was the enemy while democracy was the solution. Of course, both concepts in their extremes or when misused are harmful to society. Communism can slip into totalitarianism, while democracy can either slip into mob rule or a corporatocracy (wherein corporations buy elections in order to further their own corporate interests). To defend either extremist communism or democracy or capitalism, an extremely strong propaganda machine is necessary. Schoultz explains that in America this propaganda machine was expressed in institutions such as the Agency for International Development and the National Endowment for Democracy, which have gone on to propagandize for the spread of America's "values" to Latin America once the Cold War ended. The book is structured chronologically, beginning with the War of 1898 through the Cold War through the Cuba dilemma and through to the present day. One drawback of this book is that it is very heavy on quotations. In other words most paragraphs are interrupted by quotes from various sources; this breaks up the narrative, and makes it difficult to follow the story or to draw conclusions from the details. There is hardly a single paragraph without at least one 2-3 line quote in it. Parts that are summaries of history rather than quotes are pretty hard-hitting, like this one: "FDR had handed Smedley Butler a Medal of Honor for killing two hundred Haitian *cacos*..." (112). While it is disorienting to find so many quotes crammed into a book, it is reassuring as well, as clearly the author did comprehensive research and found every bit of relevant evidence on this controversial topic.

This book should be required reading for any U.S. politician who is about to argue for becoming entangled with Latin American politics. We have to know what happened when we intervened previously to decide how we should act in our present. Since Trump has been arguing that Mexico should pay for a wall between our countries, hopefully he will read this text (perhaps his first book in decades) to understand why his administration is continuing some of these paternalistic donations of resources and propagandistic deployment. If America is supposed to be focusing on "America First" and on helping itself, why is it continuing to hotly fight in Iraq and Afghanistan and its cold propaganda campaign in Latin America? The answers are in these pages, and the information will not surrender itself without work being put in through close reading.

Brilliant and Unique Critique of the Ties Between the Crown and the East India Company

Rupali Mishra. *A Business of State: Commerce, Politics, and the Birth of the East India Company*. 412pp, 6X9". ISBN: 978-0-674-98456-1. Cambridge: Harvard University Press, 2018.

****

I requested this book because I have been coming across mentions of the East India Company in my research into eighteenth century British literature. Travel voyage novels and various other fictional and true accounts touch on it directly or indirectly as it had sway over the world's economy and politics at its peak in 1800. This book is not entirely what would have been directly relevant for my research, as it covers the birth of the company in 1600 and its history in its first century. Regardless, its founding has more profound lessons than its later history as its foundational structure is unique to history. The cover explains that the "monarch and his privy counselors" as well as an "extended cast of eminent courtiers and powerful merchants" shaped the nature of this company. Mishra's analysis is distinguished from earlier studies as she argues that the East India Company was "embedded within—and inseparable from—the state" in contrast with earlier interpretations of it as a "private entity" that became state-like. This is a particularly important distinction for my own research because as a part of the state, this company had the power to commission propagandistic novels and other accounts that glorified its colonial endeavors. The controversial thesis is particularly impressive as the book was authored by only an Assistant Professor in the Department of History at Auburn University (without an extensive publication record or decades of teaching experience). The text is of the highest quality, with polished prose and detailed notes, so it is clear why Harvard University Press accepted it.

The content is divided into categories of people or entities that governed the Company, including the Court of Committees, merchants, adventurers, and the regime. Other chapters look at separate decades and how the relationship between the Crown and the Company changed, including a chapter on trade manipulation in the 1630s. the first page opens with the central argument that was made in a "questionably legal" memo: "Each of the schemes... involved the transfer of money from Company members to the monarch." These schemes involved lending money to his Majesty, allowing his Majesty to collect fines on the adventurers participating in the trade, and still others offered a 10% interest loan from the Monarch to the Company. All of these schemes are as relevant to today's problems as they were in this period. We are currently debating the legality of a presidential American official accepting a loan at extremely favorable terms in exchange for offering a military government position. Perhaps, understanding how antiquated and engrained this type of corruption is in our western political system will help us to solve our current problems.

This book does a great job of explaining all of the basic concepts covered, allowing a reader unfamiliar with this topic to gradually understand it without checking outside sources. For example, the section "Patents and Trading Companies" begins with a summary of England's trade relationships that existed before the foundation of the Company, namely that its "biggest export crop was wool" sold "primarily to the Low Countries." The Company opened many new doors and built up the most economic power. Other companies like the Somers Island Company (founded in 1615) and the Royal Africa Company (1618) are hardly mentioned. Each of these companies had a geographic name because the monarch granted them patents that allowed them exclusive trading rights in a given geographical area. In other words, they were government-imposed monopolies (19). Anybody in England with a ship might have wanted to engage in independent trade with East India, but only this single company was allowed to do so across England. Given the current climate of consolidation or mergers among corporations, we seem to be headed back to this monopolistic pattern. The monopolization of trade with East India occurred because earlier traders lost a lot of money in sunk ships and other misadventures, so consolidation was sold by Elizabeth I as a form of protection against individual losses (25).

The wealth of information in this book is astounding given the complexity and rarity of sources from this period. This is recommended reading for anybody involved in business or government, and not only for historians (students and professors alike) in this field.

A Welcoming Biography of a Brilliant Composer

David Schiff. *Carter: The Master Musicians*. $34.95: hardcover. 266pp, 6X9". ISBN: 978-0-19-025915-0. Oxford: Oxford University Press, 2018.

****

This is a rare biography of a recent American classical music composer, Elliott Carter. The book pays particular attention to Carter's "politically charged Depression-era ballets" as well as his personal works that were affected by his family life. The story is based on Carter's personal sketches and letters. It is chronologically organized by decades out of Carter's life, though some chapters veer off into themes like vehicular accidents and farewell symphonies. The "Author's Note" opens with a statement that this is the author's third book about Carter's music, as his first work on this subject was *The Music of Elliott Carter* (1983). David Schiff is a composer himself, who studied under Carter at Juilliard School. Chapter One opens with another curious fact: Carter was 104 when he died; this explains the relatively "mature" age of the author, his pupil. The pair first met in 1971 when Schiff was pursuing a doctorate at Columbia in English literature. Carter began making music in 1928, releasing 150 published musical pieces, of which "half, including his only opera, were completed after he turned ninety" (1). Chapter Three ends with a very helpful summary of Carter's C.V., which lists his place and time of birth and death, his marriage, son, education, at Harvard, and his employment, which started at the Ballet Caravan in 1937, and included teaching at St. John's College, working at the Office of War Information, the Peabody Conservatory, and then later teaching at Columbia, Queens College, Yale, Cornell, and Juilliard until 1985. Carter picked up on his musical publishing after retiring from teaching. Only the Julliard position lasted for a couple of decades, whereas the other jobs lasted for a year or two on a "short-lived and part-time" basis (25). The rest of the book expands on each of these and many other accomplishments from this curious life. A rich collection of details about everything that can be known about Carter has been collected, digested and presented to readers. The center of the book offers a dozen black and white photographs of Carter in various social settings. The back of the book also offers a helpful "Personalia" section, wherein the biographies of the key persons that Carter interacted with are offered.

This is a welcoming and pleasant biography of a unique and admired composer that allows a glimpse into this cloistered world. Anybody who is interested in the musical profession should read this book. It might make a good addition to a course about musical composition or a special course about Carter. Academic libraries can definitely benefit from having this work in their collections in case somebody is researching modern composers.

Misinformation and Misdirection on Surprise

Vera Tobin. *Elements of Surprise: Our Mental Limits and the Satisfactions of Plot.* 332pp. ISBN: 978-0-674-98020-4. Cambridge: Harvard University Press, 2018.

***

This book promises to explain to researchers and authors alike the elements that make up a successful narrative surprise. Isn't surprise just something that you did not expect? Apparently not. Obviously, every author who wants to enter the popular fiction or screenplay writing arenas has to know how to deliver a surprise ending, with a few mini-surprises along the way. If the ending is entirely predictable and a fictitious work is entirely formulaic, the whole thing will appear to replay the same work the viewer has seen countless times before. The mystery and romance genres nowadays are hyper-formulaic; this restricts what is likely to happen in them in the beginning, middle and end. But something about the plot still has to be surprising to avoid audiences walking out. Tobin does not only review the pop genres, but also looks into how surprise works in classics and "obscure literature". The cover explains that surprise "works by taking advantage of our mental limits." This is pretty cryptic, but hopefully Tobin surprises readers within by delivering on this mighty goal. Does this mean that surprise is difficult for the feeble-minded to grasp? The cover goes on: "*Elements of Surprise* describes how cognitive biases, mental shortcuts, and quirks of memory conspire with stories to produce wondrous illusions…" In my research into surprise in mystery novels, I learned that many mysteries use tricks by introducing new information that was never touched on in the novel to create a surprise; in other words, most of these mysteries cannot be solved by even the closest and most astute reader; but, this book seems to argue that the information is provided in these novels but is obscured by memory. I doubt this book is seriously intended for fiction writers as the cover promises because the chapter titles are pretty cryptic as well: "The Naming of Things" and "When Unreliability Is a Surprise". If an author wants to create a practical guide, typically chapter and section titles are very revealing, taking the reader by the hand and leading him or her to the exact bits of information needed to achieve a story element. The "Introduction" fails to give a clear explanation of this argument, veering into "a state of not-knowing" and the "curse of knowledge", concepts that are common in nonsensical linguistic studies, and should not enter into helpful practical guides on how to create surprise. If the reader knows what the surprise was and how he or she feels about it afterwards psychologically is hardly helpful to the author, who is interested in the moment of surprise and achieving a satisfying climax and resolution. The next sub-section of the "Introduction" begins somewhat rationally by summarizing the surprising elements in Othello's plot (that Iago is really a villain), but instead of classifying and dissecting why and how this is surprising, the author then discusses how "inaccessible Desdemona's subjective experience is." What does this have to do with the promised subject of this book? The author is digesting Stanley Cavell's essay on this topic here rather than presenting her own argument, so it all becomes even more confusing and irrelevant. The paragraph ends with a quote of the word "riddle", but other than a brief note on "skepticism" the rest of the paragraph barely touches on anything surprising (6-7). As I thought might happen, there's a whole chapter seriously dedicated to smartness with sections like "Smart Stuff", "Or Not So Smart" and "Mental Contamination and the Illusion of Knowledge". The latter chapter seems to be especially insulting? Mental contamination? The opening paragraph explains in part that this all has to do with who knows what; for example, if a character presents a "deceptive viewpoint" that leads readers to misinterpret what happened until this deception is revealed in a surprise ending. But instead of breaking down clearly how to create this deception, the section then repeats the same idea, making it more and more convoluted: "We forget things we once knew, conflate or distort past experiences, and even remember events that never happened" (76-7). What do these commonly known things have to do with the elements of surprise? It is related to the general idea of what is known and unknow, but when these types of things are repeated in every paragraph with slight variations but without moving the explanation anywhere, they become nonsensical. Somebody really should have edited these repetitions out. Occasionally, the narrative does break into a logical and clear rhetoric. For example, in the section on "Burying Information", the author offers a list of specific techniques that can achieve this: "Mention the item as little as possible"; "Use linguistic structures which have been shown empirically to reduce prominence (e.g. embed a mention of the item within a subordinate clause)." The second of these is particularly relevant because the author of this book actively practices burying her meanings within these pages. She creates long and convoluted sentences to hide the repetitions and the nuggets of wisdom her research has gathered. If she is doing this consciously, it's difficult to guess why a scholarly author would want to surprise or confuse readers... This list also suggests offering the most relevant information in places where the reader has lost interest or is "distracted." This definitely happens in convoluted studies like this one; the opening chapters and paragraphs at the start of a chapter are intended to be as dull as possible to lull readers into losing concentration when the bits of helpful information are presented deep within a paragraph without any introductory remark to specify that it offers a payoff. The other trick she is using is: "Make it difficult for the reader to make inferences by splitting up information needed to make the inferences" (114). By interrupting the explanations with returns to her contemplations about "knowing" and "not-knowing" and other bits of nonsense, Tobin is breaking up the pieces of information needed to bring the relevant bits of evidence and argument together into a coherent whole.

If you want to know how to create extremely convoluted scholarly essays or books to substitute repetitions for thorough research, you will definitely find what you are looking for in these pages (if you can stay with it long enough to reap the rewards). And if you are a pop, formulaic fiction writer interested in learning about linguistic and structural tricks for burying clues in a way that will leave readers bewildered, clueless, confused and disoriented, it might be worth your while to dig into this study as well. But if you are a member of the public casually interested in surprise, stay away from this book if you value your peace of mind. It's going to disturb, confuse and misguide you.

A Reader on Fictitious Lies of All Sorts

Nick Marx & Matt Sienkiewics, eds. *The Comedy Studies Reader*. $29.95. 314pp, 6X9", 12 images. ISBN: 978-1-4773-1600-9. Austin: University of Texas Press, August 1, 2018.

***

This reader promises to explain the enormous field of comedy. Back in the days of Greek theater, all of fiction was pretty much divided into comedies and tragedies, and most plots written today also tend to fall into one of these two categories. Even if something isn't funny, it can be comedic if it has a happy ending and other elements inherent to this category. So, it is a very ambitious task to gather all of the major thoughts on comedy in a single book. The essays included consider "the carnivalesque, comedy mechanics and absurdity, psychoanalysis, irony, genre, race and ethnicity, gender and sexuality, and nation and globalization." It is puzzling what the relationship between the nation and comedy might be; perhaps this signifies a discussion of political comedy. The two canonical authors included are my archenemies: Mikhail Bakhtin and Sigmund Freud. The latter I dislike because of his chauvinist perspectives: saying that every woman has penis-envy is insulting, and I'm sure Freud had vagina-envy if he came up with this hacked idea. The book also promises to explain comedy's "evolution" into a "myriad subgenres". The two authors are media and communications professors. The book opens with a joke on the page across from the title page: fig 1. includes a figure and a hand holding a pie, and fig 2. shows the pie heading towards the unmoved, smiling face. This is an inside joke for academics accustomed to seeing figures in scholarly books. There are a few stills, posters and other small black and white images in other parts of the book. Essays by canonical authors are mixed in with recent scholarship as the book is divided by topics such as the carnivalesque, comedy mechanics & absurdity, psychoanalyzing comedy, irony, genre and the like. Some of these essays look at individual films such as *Family Guy, The Big Bang Theory, SNL,* or *Rush Hour 2.* One chapter's introduction is named after a comedian, Amy Schumer (the one on gender and sexuality). Freud's chapters are called "Jokes and Their Relation to the Unconscious" and "Humor". The first of these is a page long and attempts to philosophically summarize jokes as things that give pleasure while also insulting without the social stigma otherwise associated with insults.

Because so many varied essays are presented, it is difficult to summarize the essence of any reader. Some of the essays are heavy on citations, while others rely on theoretical reflections. The introduction to the first chapter on the "Carnivalesque" begins with a couple of pages from a screenplay, which ends thus: "Frank's pee returns louder than ever: He lets out a loud fart. The mayor sits down, defeated" (17-8). Well, what can be concluded from this? How do the authors conclude this section? Thus: "carnivalesque comedy becomes an important way for us to collectively confront unimaginable acts of tragedy" (19). This brings me back to my initial pondering on this topic: if there are only two types of fiction, comedies and tragedies, and if comedy is a way of confronting tragedy, well, then, clearly this book could have been called: *A Reader on Fictitious Lies of All Sorts.*

Insightful Guide to Environmental Issues with the Giant Ogallala Aquifer

John Opie, Char Miller, and Kenna Lang Archer. *Ogallala: Water for a Dry Land: Third Edition.* $35. 438pp, 6X9", 18 images. ISBN: 978-0-8032-9697-8. Lincoln: Nebraska University Press, August 1, 2018.

****

This is a study of the Ogallala aquifer, an underground water reserve that stretches between South Dakota to Texas. The southern tip of it is a bit over an hour from my house, so it seemed like an interesting topic to look into. It developed from glacial melts from the Rocky Mountains. It promises to be an environmental history and a geography. Somehow it also manages to wander into the settlement of this area, dryland and industrial farming, and irrigation technologies. This is the third edition of this book, which has added on the previous version discussions of long-term drought, groundwater management districts' regulations, and the failure of a water capturing aquifer for Texas' urban areas. Three environmental history professors co-wrote this project. The story is somewhat chronological as the first chapter is called "The First Half-Billion Years" and the second chapter spans between 1870 and 1940. The book is full of illustrated maps that show drought patterns and groundwater districts in relation to the aquifer, as well as photos of farmers from this region at work. The stated goal for the book is to "inform and persuade" rather than solely to offer information on these topics. The significance of Ogallala is that it is "the largest underground body of fresh water in the United States." It is a non-renewable (unlike "most water supplies" in the world), so it's called "fossil water." This body is three dimensionally large, as it goes up to 300 feet in depth (1).

This made me curious to find out if my water comes from this Ogallala aquifer, so I looked it up. It was not an easy search. I came across an article about the residents of Quanah losing their water because of a main line water break. I actually didn't have water for three days so far this summer. The Judge of Hardeman county told me that their lines break at least a couple of times every year when the weather gets hot and the pipes expand and otherwise experience a lot of stress. They have limited funds for fixing problems until a major issue occurs. The one document I found that discusses sources of water for this region is the "Gateway Groundwater Conservation District Management Plan". A map on their website seems to indicate that my house in Quanah falls under the Seymour Aquifer district that spans the eastern half of the county, but the description might indicate that occasionally water comes from further away if this source is insufficient. A table that details water boundaries for the area shows that Ogallala is one of the utilized aquifers, but a minor one. Still it is possible that sometimes I receive water from the Ogallala, or groundwater somewhat similar to it in soil characteristics, so I might return to this book next time I'm having water issues. Since I am interested in local politics, it seems impossible that this book would not be helpful in the future, as, for example, it includes a discussion of State Senator Troy Fraser's debate with farmers regarding intervention and lawsuit threats "over the right to unrestricted pumping," a debate that the farmers won (196). Hardeman commissioners frequently mention water pumping out of the ground and other water related issues at their meetings. This is a very rural area where farming is still a top industry unlike in the bulk of the rest of America. Every page is filled with other critical controversies for the region like the installation of Eco-Drip on sixty thousand acres (292) and limiting consumption from the aquifer (342).

This book should be of great help to residents, farmers, and politicians across the enormous region provided for by this enormous aquifer. Scholars of environmentalist history should also be able to mine it for useful and insightful information.

A Well of Knowledge on Native American Land Diplomacy

David Bernstein. *How the West Was Drawn: Mapping, Indians, and the Construction of the Trans-Mississippi West.* $65: hardcover. 324pp, 6X9", 54 images. ISBN: 978-0-8032-4930-1. Lincoln: Nebraska University Press, August 1, 2018.

****

This is a history of land conflicts between the Pawnee, Iowa and Lakota Native Americans and the European and American settlers in the Great Plains in the eighteenth and nineteenth centuries. The unique element in this study is that Bernstein proposes that this conflict was "collaborative", wherein the native people played an equal role rather than merely responded to aggression by the settlers. He argues that the Pawnees and Iowas diplomatically negotiated for autonomy with fur traders, merchants, explorers and other agents and neighboring tribes. Curiously, I just did an interview with Michele Stephens about the Hu-

ichol people in Mexico, and she explained that the natives in Mexico
do not have equivalent reservation lands to the ones in United States.
So, it seems American natives did succeed in gaining territory through
diplomacy. Given this, it seems the story of oppression and conquer
of the natives in the U.S. is unfairly skewed towards the power of the
conquerors rather than the power of those who carved out power for
themselves despite military disadvantages. With a third of this long
book taken up with notes, numerous explanatory maps, and intricate
research throughout, this is a trustworthy source of information on this
controversial topic. One drawback is that there are only six chapters ad
they are not very clearly organized. The second half is clear enough:
it's about the cultural and science creation and destruction of "Indian
Country." But the third part includes a chapter called "The Metaphys-
ics of Indian Naming". Whenever the term "metaphysics" appears in a
history or literary studies book, typically nonsense is about to enter the
discussion… Thankfully, this chapter does not begin with nonsensical
repetitions, but rather with a concrete story of General Harney's expedi-
tion against the Sioux Indians (197), so the title is more of an academic
joke than a description of its theoretical leanings. A subsection in this
chapter is called "The Science of Nation Building" and it describes the
significance of a detailed 1853-5 survey that made some of this western
land real for potential settlers; in other words, this is very concrete and
specific research rather than a conceptional digression. This history is
written with plenty of dramatic tension and consideration for helping
readers stay interested in the narrative. For example, the "Introduction"
opens with the story surrounding the controversy about the first map
of where Native American tribes held territories just before Columbus
arrived by Aaron Carapella called, *Map of our Tribal Nations: Our Own
Names and Original Locations*, which came out only in 2012, just a few
years ago. The controversy was the misspellings of the supposedly origi-
nal names (not those they are commonly known by today) that Aaron
gathered on his travels to archives and different native sites, as well as
several other inaccuracies scholars found in this map once it became a
bestseller and garnered him national media attention. This story helps
to explain how contentious any discussion about Native American land
boundaries has been.

　　This is a great source of easily accessible information that would
otherwise take a researcher months of archival research to gather to-
gether. Bernstein has done the work for you. This research is also well

polished and written up in a way that is a pleasure to read. Anybody who is engaged in researching Native Americans across both the north and south American contents should find a well of helpful information in this study.

Annotated Retellings of the Stabbing of Chief Crazy Horse

Robert A. Clark, Ed; Commentary by Carroll Friswold. *The Killing of Chief Crazy Horse, Bison Classic Edition. Three eyewitness views by the Indian, Chief He Dog, the Indian white, William Garnett, and the white doctor, Valentine McGillycubby.* $19.95. 150pp, 5.5X8.5", 14 images. ISBN: 978-1-4962-0057-0. Lincoln: Nebraska University Press, October 1, 2018.

****

For anybody interested in American history, the story of the fatal wounding of Oglala Sioux chief Crazy Horse in a scene strikingly similar to recent police shootings on unarmed African American man is a great treat. The shooting did not happen when Chief Crazy Horse finally surrendered after a lengthy rebellion at the end of the Battle of the Little Big Horn. The story is told from three perspectives in a manner that matches some of the best murder mysteries. Whodunnit? Aside from who fired the weapon, the question of why they fired without an obvious provocation is in the center of this conspiracy. A possible culprit might be found among the other Native American chiefs that thought Crazy Horse was receiving favors from the U.S. Army for his surrender. Did these chiefs or a U.S. spy spread rumors that Crazy Horse was planning a new rebellion? The stabbing with a bayonet happened when Crazy Horse was being arrested in Fort Robinson, Nebraska on September 5 under suspicion of stirring a new uprising. Curiously, after discussing the potential threat the other chiefs had towards Crazy Horse, a chief narrator, Chief He Dog is described as "the victim's friend and lifelong companion." Does this leave room for doubt about Chief Dog's narrative as well? Could he have been tempted into telling falsehoods or threatened into a narrative that insufficiently exonerated Crazy Horse? The second narrator of this event is

William Garnett, the "guide and interpreter for Lieutenant William P. Clark, on special assignment to General Crook," the general in charge of the military maneuvers involved. The last storyteller is Valentine McGillycuddy, "the medical officer who attended Crazy Horse in his last hours." The narratives are promised to deliver "all the starkness and horror of classic tragedy." One of the editors of this volume, Robert A. Clark, is the editor in chief of Washington State University Press, and curiously shares a last name with one of the narrators and an imprint he formally published, Arthur H. Clark Co., though there might not be any real relation between these. His co-editor is Carroll Friswold, a writer and editor into related subjects. A large part of this book is taken up with their introductions and commentaries on the brief letters and accounts from these primary sources. The preface to this edition explains that this collection was previously released from the Arthur H. Clark Company, edited by one of these editors, which sold 300 copies that it printed, a success that inspired the University of Nebraska Press to make this project available to a wider audience. The original version was edited by Mr. Friswold, and Robert A. Clark, the current editor, isn't shy about finding some faults with the original commentary, including "his support of the authenticity of the photograph of Crazy Horse" (xvii). The book has pretty wide margins, so it is easier to read than even the page count suggests. Five photos of the depicted characters is presented in the center. One criticism that comes to mind is that the letters from William Garnett lack the details that might truly uncover the great mystery that the cover promises. There are just a few short letters that describe the battle before the stabbing more so than the stabbing itself. More room is given to another chief, Red Cloud, for whom Garnett interpreted than to the protagonist. They also discuss the narrator wishing he had had his picture taken with Crazy Horse, and questioning the spelling of his name (67). Then again, some of the later letters reveal some curious bits: Lieut. Lemly states that Crazy Horse was arrested because he and Louis Richards daughter had run away and lived together, and that Crazy Horse would not give her up" (75). That's definitely a strong motive for murder (on the part of the girl's family, considering racist sentiments of the period). The narrative of Chief He Dog was "written down by his son Rev. Eagle Hawk, Oglala, S. Dak" and it begins with stating the four rules every Indian chief has to keep. It continues in this philosophical vein, offering details from the surrounding events as well as reflections on their greater meanings.

Few sources like these have been digitized by archivists and a 300-copies printing probably means that it would not be available even through interlibrary loan in most places, so it's great that Nebraska published this general public version. This book should make for great supplemental reading for a high school or a college history class. It can also be useful for a research paper on Native American history, or even for a paper on recent police brutality cases. There cannot be enough books like this that digs out treasures from the dusty archives, so the rest of us don't have to travel to Nebraska to discover them.

A Biased Review of the Kosovo "Stabilization" from within the Ranks

Sean M. Maloney; Foreword by Sir Mike Jackson. *Operation Kinetic: Stabilizing Kosovo*. $38.95: hardcover. 512pp, 6X9", 17 images. ISBN: 978-1-61234-964-0. Lincoln: Potomac Books: Nebraska University Press, July 1, 2018.

***

This is a study of NATO's and especially the Canadian Army's 1990s work of stabilizing Kosovo and the former Yugoslav Republic of Macedonia after this region suffered from genocide and other atrocities. Why did NATO enter this conflict? What exactly did they do while they were there? Kosovo appears frequently in news broadcasts and in other media channels, but other than the atrocities references, it is a topic that is hazy in my imagination. The cover explains that international troops performed "surveillance" and sent in units that worked to prevent "violence" that might have resulted in further bloodshed if the Serbian Army had to be called in. The second chapter in the background section describes the long history of the conflict in Kosovo, spanning from 1389 to 1999, when the central military conflict related occurred. The "Foreword" by Sir Mike Jackson describes Canada's involvement from the first-person perspective of a commander that led NATO's Allied Command Europe Rapid Reaction Corps up to the pivotal year, 1999, when in March NATO started air strikes against Yugoslavia as peace talks failed. Yugoslavia "conceded on June 3, and this commander led the Kumanovo talks "with a Serb military delegation." They secured Serb withdrawal. Then they stayed to assure "demilitarization," securing the "volatile and angry population; restarting public utilities…; providing support to UNMIK, the UN civil administration; assuring freedom of movement; demining; assisting with the return of refugees; and deterring any reoccupation of Kosovo by Former Republic of Yugoslavia (FRY) forces" (xi-xii). This helps to explain some of the tasks involved in this peacekeeping and hot fighting process. Then, the main author explains in the "Acknowledgements" that he was involved in this conflict as a historian for 4 Canadian Mechanized Brigade. Since both of them have been and continue to be employed by the military or its branches, one criticism is that their views must be biased by this proximity. If they were not biased they might have started this discussion by explaining why and how the intervention became necessary, and questioning the need to engage in a violent conflict abroad. Is there really any logical justification for firing a weapon in war or peace? These types of questions do not come up if career military personnel are authoring their own war stories. The historian does mention that September 11, 2001 "overshadowed" his work on this book, if not the Kosovo conflict, but was there a relationship between Kosovo and 9/11; would the latter have happened if America did not become entangled in Kosovo and other similar conflicts in the Middle East and other hot zones? The introduction begins like an action movie with a description of troops swarming "onto the sleep eight-wheeled armored vehicles, attaching equipment, mounting machine guns, tightening bolts, and filling jerry cans with that precious fluid, water" (xix). Usually, I enjoy reading very active historical descriptions, but this history is a bit too close to the present, so it makes me pretty uncomfortable to be entertained by this drama. The first chapter begins by raising the question that is clouding my own judgment on this matter, "'Why do we bother? They've been killing each other for hundreds (or thousands of years anyway.'" The answer given in this section is that Canada became involved to "prevent spillover effects on adjacent countries, and to forestall aggressive Russian intervention in the region that would affect NATO and therefore Canada" (4). Whenever Russia is blamed for international warfare, I always imagine that Russia is being used as a scapegoat to hide corruption at the heart of all warfare. NATO and Russia have renewed their conflicts in 2014 when Russian annexed Crimea from Ukraine. I published a couple of novels by one of the leaders of the Ukrainian revolution, so I know a bit about this conflict. The annexation seems absurd and more like a symbolic grab rather than as a military threat. We are hardly still in the age of colonialism when a non-democratic annexation of foreign entities can be executed without sanction by the public in one's own country. It seems more likely that warfare is an excuse for contractors to make billions in arms, military equipment and other deals. Wars provide jobs for commanders and their historians. Ukraine is a third world country. Why would any ruler be interested in annexing even its richest part like Crimea? The Soviet Union collapsed because of the financial pressures involved in carrying so many indebted and impoverished Eastern European countries. Why would Russia want to renew these expensive unions? Would all of these questions be answered if I read this book cover-to-cover? At the moment the thought of making the attempt is too depressing. Whenever I meet an American person that otherwise does not know who I am, they always only ask me where I'm from and after I say I am from Russia, they do not ask me anything else. The Cold War-style anti-Russian sentiment I've faced as a refugee in America over the last three decades has been very annoying, so from my perspective reading an entire book of anti-Russian propaganda is akin to an African American reading a book of anti-African American propaganda authored by the KKK. I do not agree with Russia's annexation of Crimea nor with its anti-gay laws nor the various other illogical decisions Russia has taken since I left at the fall of the Soviet Union, but if I'm viewed as the enemy without being at fault for Russia's decisions, it is difficult to see Russia as a viable enemy as a whole entity. If somebody is reading this and they would like to understand the Kosovo conflict better to have something to complain about Russia on, this is definitely a great source for you. And if I ever decide to write something concrete about Kosovo, I will definitely return to attempt to concur this book once again.

Hilariously Offensive Study of Rude Settlers in a Rugged Mexican Landscape

Martin Austin Nesvig. *Promiscuous Power: An Unorthodox History of New Spain*. $45: hardcover. 268pp, 6X9", 11 images. ISBN: 978-1-4773-1582-8. Austin: University of Texas Press, June 2, 2018.

This is an innovative perspective on the conquest of Mexico as a project accomplished by "local agents—magistrates, bureaucrats, parish priests, ranchers, miners, sugar producers", who established the empire, hardly aware of the grand plans of their monarchy back in Europe. Instead of looking at the whole country, this is study of the Michoacan province in western Mexico. From this perspective, the conquest was primarily economically motivated as self-interested individuals worked to better their own lives. Most curiously, Nesvig challenges the often-repeated notion that Spanish Catholicism succeeded in capturing the region by suppressing indigenous cultures. Nesvig presents the opposite picture wherein the focal province allowed European settlers to leave their own Catholicism behind in favor of a lawless, decentralized system akin to anarchy. Martin Austin Nesvig is an associate professor of history at the University of Miami, who has authored and edited a few boos on related topics. One of the chapters is called, "'I Shit on You, Sir'; or, A Rather Unorthodox Lot of Catholics Who Didn't Fear the Inquisition". Even if one of the characters in this history used the word "shit" in an archival document, it says something about Nesvig if he utilized this phrase in a chapter title. It is definitely unique in the scholarly genre… It might have been funnier if all of the chapters had slang in them… and indeed another chapter has the word "Murderous Dudes" in it… Then, he goes on to open the "Acknowledgements" with a self-reflective observation: "Acknowledgements in academic books are fascinating reading, but the form is a little strange…" (ix). Indeed it is, especially if it opens thus, and then proceeds with a thanks to his partner instead of inserting this note at the end, as the formula for "Acknowledgements" dictates. Then, also somewhat oddly, there is a "Cast of Characters", but instead of full biographies, it just gives the characters brief descriptions like bishop, imposter, royal judge and conquistador. Why not just include these descriptors next to their names in the text? The "Introduction" returns to a more formulaic format for such studies as it describes the "physical beauty" of the nature in the Michoacan region (1). The photos of the region in later pages do not do justice to this as they depict a lonely church or a stack of rocks (the ruins of the Purepecha ritual complex), but perhaps the color versions are more inspiring. For some reason, the ruins include a spelled-out link to its Wikipedia page; the current convention is to leave such links out, as they can be found by typing the name of the image into a search engine. Some regional art and several maps also illustrate this book.

This book should interest liberal-minded historians and students interested in the colonization of Mexico. Ardent Catholics are unlikely to be at all pleased with the contents or findings of this study, and might be offended by some of it. Perhaps Mexicans (native and descendants of the colonists) might be offended by it as well. Maybe pretty much everybody will find something to be offended by in these pages. On the bright side, anybody who is not easily offended, and more easily amused is likely to enjoy reading this controversial and non-conformist study.

Dramatic True Crime Detective Stories

Thomas A. Reppetto. *American Detective: Behind the Scenes of Famous Criminal Investigations.* $34.95: hardcover. 312pp, 6X9", 20 images. ISBN: 978-1-64012-022-8. Lincoln: Nebraska University Press, August 1, 2018.

****

This is a series of case studies of police detectives' top cases in America in the 1920-70s decades. I found this book particularly helpful in learning a bit more about practical policing for an anti-police procedural mystery novel, *Fatal Design*, I was finishing when I was reading it. My story took place in Los Angeles, so the LAPD chapter was especially relevant. This book glorifies detectives and makes them appear super-human. The cover advertises these decades as the pinnacle of policing, whereas many might see it as a time when police forces were especially violent towards African Americans and other minorities, and this brutality went unchecked. The decline of the status of detectives after the 1970s might have been due to more strenuous reporting that uncovered corruption and problems with cases, as well as the entry of scientific or forensic studies into policing that substituted detectives' hunches with fingerprint or DNA evidence. Still, it should be of interest to all citizens and police members alike to read the details of successful investigations from a period that was somewhat pre-scientific. How did detectives solve cases back then? What tools, tricks and methods did they use that modern police and mystery writers can acquire? The detectives covered are Thad Brown (Black Dahlia murder in Los Angeles), Elliott Ness (corruption investigator, but failure at catching the "Mad Butcher" that decapitated over a dozen victims), and J. Edgar Hoover ("top cop" at the head of the FBI).

The author, Thomas A. Reppetto, is a former commander of detectives in the Chicago Police Department with a PhD from Harvard, and an added history of work as a professor and vice president at the John Jay College of Criminal Justice. He has also been active in government, serving as the head of the Citizens Crime Commission of New York City. With a background like this, obviously Reppetto is biased on the side of detectives, but his work in academia must have given him distance from this world, and he isn't afraid to look at the dirty components of the job.

A dozen archival photographs from across America's detective history is provided in the middle of the book, starting with Allan Pinkerton (who founded one of the first detection agencies) pictured with Abraham Lincoln. Every part of this book is written like a mystery novel, beginning in the most exciting and shocking part of the story and then returning to the details. The endings typically reveal whodunnit or explain why an investigation failed. So it reads like a mystery short stories collection, or a bit better than average mysteries due to the added heavy research that layers numerous details onto the dramatic plot. Because the stories cover various states and time periods they jump between a 1920s Texas cowboys train robbery that was solved by Chicago's police, to a 1930s armored-car heist in Brooklyn, to a 1950 Brink's holdup in Boston that nearly reached its statute of limitations because of squabbles between police and FBI forces (xxvii). The first chapter does a good job of placing this period in greater historic background by reviewing the rice of detectives from the Civil War to the 1920s. Policing itself was not much older with the first police department being founded in Boston in 1838. Throughout the book, there are plenty of stones being thrown around as to who might be to blame for various failures to deliver a suspect, as happens here: "The feeling among the Hudson County crew was that the Somerset team had not conducted a thorough investigation..." (61).

Great set of dramatic true crime retellings written for general readers and policing researchers alike.

A Delightful Submarine of Propaganda for Roosevelt and the American Military

Matthew Oyos. *In Command: Theodore Roosevelt and the American Military*. $36.95: hardcover. 456pp, 6X9", 13 images. ISBN: 978-1-61234-967-1. Lincoln: Nebraska University Press, August 1, 2018.

****

This is a study of the work Theodore Roosevelt did to strengthen the U.S. military in his eight-year presidency that did not see a major war (1901-9). Particular attention is given to Roosevelt's innovations in technology, militia, and international missions. The "Introduction" opens with a lesson in Roosevelt's sense of "civic duty" as he volunteered to fight Spaniards and became a hero during a battle on July 1, 1898, returning in the middle of a violent fight to rally his men and to overtake a high point that secured America a victory. This indicates that this is a book that is glorifying warfare and making a connection between pride in one's country and military service. The chapters are divided chronologically and by major themes in Roosevelt's military policies. Some of the story takes readers back to his days at the Naval War College, and as a member of the Rough Riders, but most of it looks at his time in office. There are some digressions throughout into other bits of Roosevelt's biography than the military. For example, a section discusses how Roosevelt's public relations team staged "hikes and hunts" for him to "reinforce… an image of ruggedness and vigor" (103). Other parts look at individual small innovations that Roosevelt brought in such as the introduction of a row of dummies that those training in the army could hit to mimic hitting bodies in actual warfare (185). Chapters are helpfully broken down into sections that should help researchers find relevant information. For example under chapter 6's broad title "In the Fullness of It All", the sections are called: "Mechanic in Chief" (on Roosevelt's interest and contributions to various types of military designs), "Innovator in Chief" (on his operation and testing of risky new mechanisms, such as driving a submarine on one of his vacations) and "Big Guns for the Big Stick" (on Roosevelt's lobbying of Congress to approve more ship and other military building). Roosevelt did not only war with Congress over military spending, but he also faced opposition on various other fronts. One of these instances was an "eruption over Roosevelt's handling of the Brownsville affair… in 1906". This incident centered against the accusation that "African American troops had shot up Brownsville, Texas." The section name "Brownsville" attracted my attention to this part because I lived for a year in Brownsville when I taught at UTRGV; it's at the southern-most tip of Texas, on the Mexican border. Roosevelt "summarily dis-missed" 167 soldiers "from service" from among the accused African Americans. Tensions initially sparked because of segregation rules. The author attempts to garner sympathy for Roosevelt despite his ques-tionable actions, explaining that Roosevelt had condemned lynching and had met with Booker T. Washington in his first months in office. Roosevelt is called a "chief disrupter" and "preacher militant" (excus-ing his behavior), but the conclusion to the section does confirm that it was a "wrong" on Roosevelt's part which was only corrected in 1972, when "the troopers were cleared of all charges" (266-76). Like most biographies, this work does its best to make its central character likable and appealing to readers. It is mostly pro-military and pro-Roosevelt propaganda. But, as far as propaganda goes, this is a delightful bit of it. There are a few too many speculations without sufficient evidence regarding how Roosevelt was feeling or what he was thinking (rather than a presentation of the pure facts), but these digressions do not steer too far from the main storyline so they should make for more enjoyable reading for the general public.

The Dramatic Adventures of America's First Diplomats

Peter D. Eicher. *Raising the Flag: America's First Envoys in Faraway Lands.* $36.95: hardcover. 416pp, 6X9", 40 images. ISBN: 978-1-61234-970-1. Lincoln: Nebraska University Press, August 1, 2018.

****

The first person that comes into my mind when I think of an American diplomat is Thomas Jefferson and his work as a minister to France in the crucial years around the American Revolution, wherein he man-aged to convince France to back America in the conflict against their rival monarchy, Britain. This type of diplomacy won America its independence, so America's diplomats are the underrated players in international politics. There are only so many countries that a US president can think about in a day, but these envoys can be all over the map, looking out for America's interests. Here's the summary: "Their stories, often stranger than fiction, are replete with intrigues, revolutions, riots, war, shipwrecks, swashbucklers, desperadoes, and bootleggers." Since I've traveled to China, Mexico, Italy, Israel and other countries and since I was born in Soviet Russia, I definitely can confirm that simply traveling abroad is full of drama and misadventure, representing a foreign government in an official capacity definitely adds an extreme level of danger to the job. Typically, when governments go abroad they do it with a slew of federal agents or a massive military force, but a diplomat's job is to have a minimal military presence with them as their job is avoiding wars rather than engaging in them. So, they are out there preaching for America amidst a country that might be extremely hostile to this message, and to this lone propogandist. The summary goes on: "Early envoys abroad faced hostile governments, physical privations, disease, isolation, and the daunting challenge of explaining American democracy to foreign rulers. Many suffered threats from tyrannical despots, some were held as slaves or hostages, and others led foreign armies into battle." The period examined is between the American Revolution and the Civil War. These stories shaped what we all currently accept as America's established foreign policy. The author's comments on these narratives comes from experience as he is a retired U.S. Foreign Service officer who served at various countries around the world. This is one of the most beautiful jacket designs out of the set: great painting at the center, and great use of the patriotic red, white and blue without sliding into pure formulaic flag-propaganda as it's all very elegantly executed. There are also some interesting photographs, paintings, and drawings in the center of the book.

The "Introduction" explains that Benjamin Franklin, John Adams, Thomas Jefferson and other famous diplomats were intentionally left out in favor of lesser known once that deserve to be brought into public consciousness. The first chapter begins at the start of the American Revolution with the retelling of the Boston Tea Party, wherein Americans dumped newly arrived British tea out of a ship, in a way declaring the war. The diplomat covered is Samuel Shaw who was chosen to lead America's first expedition to China to establish a tea trade to meet the demand for a product that was no longer available from Britain.

Shaw had served in the early Revolution, but had little education or travel experience. The information about this process of establishing trade with China comes primarily from Shaw's letters home. A large portion of the chapter is dedicated to explaining the political issues related to trade with China. The main problem was that Americans had very little knowledge about China's culture, history, language and the like because of the difficulty of exchanging such information across the globe in this early period. What could be traded, the prices of the trade, and other matters had to be determined. The first voyage took a lot of ginseng aboard because it was known that it is a priced commodity in China, and it grew wild in America. Various other products were taken to diversify the odds that something would sell. The difficult voyage is described in dramatic details. The approach to establishing trade is explained. Then, a major international incident, the Canton war is related: during a dinner party the British East India Company ship Lady Hughes fired a customer salute cannon shot, which accidentally killed a boatman and injured two others on a small Chinese vessel nearby. The gunman who fired the shot was detained in Chinese custody and later executed. Shaw later served in the War Department before returning to work in Chinese trade. The final pages of the chapter explain how trade gradually migrated from ginseng and into opium between these two countries, later leading to the Opium War. So, each of these chapters focuses on the biographies of the diplomats, the history of the related international contacts, and the political issues these interactions touched on.

Very engaging and a pleasure to read for casual readers and researchers alike. The research is immaculate as well as the polished writing. This is an interesting story, and the political discussions are handled gently and apparently without much bias. For example, China isn't blamed for the execution of the gunman, but neither are China's actions excused. Anybody who enjoys a great adventure narrative (fictional or true) will have fun just drifting into this set of sagas.

Intricate Maps with Encyclopedic Entries for Most of the World-Carving Treaties

Malise Ruthven, General Editor. *Carving Up the Globe: An Atlas of Diplomacy*. $39.95. 256pp. ISBN: 978-0-674-97624-5. Cambridge:

Harvard University Press, 2018.

****

This is an encyclopedia of various treaties and other types of agreements that have carved the boundaries between countries. Many of these agreements are illustrated with large maps that show where the line was drawn and which countries were affected. Geopolitical reasons for the placement are offered. Adding acres of territory has historically meant significant wealth not only for the countries but even for those making the boundary decisions. The pages are huge in size, really allowing for zoomed in and detailed map images. The maps cover a wide spectrum across the known history of the world: "ancient Egyptian and Hittite accords to the first Sino-Tibetan peace in 783 CE, the Sykes-Picot Agreement of 1916, and the 2014 Minsk Protocol looming over the war in Ukraine." Aside from simple ownership of territories, these maps also illustrate "missile and nuclear pacts, environmental treaties, chemical weapons conventions, and economic deals". The motivations behind these treaties are explained in the commentary, with a focus on empire-building, security, and national wealth. All of this complex and divergent information is edited together by Malise Ruthven, a former editor with the BBC Arabic Service and World Service in London. The book is organized chronologically, starting with the Treaty of Mesilim from 2550 BCE, the first treaty in the world that was entered into the historic record (as it was around this time when written texts first started appearing). It was between two kingdoms and settled the matter of an irrigation canal and a land boundary. It refers to one of the kings, Enlil as "father of the gods". It is illustrated with a colorful map that shows the various kingdoms, tribes and other entities that crowded into a narrow territory around the Persian Gulf and the main rivers running into it. It is a bit difficult to tell from this map where the irrigation canal in question is, and the boundaries between countries seems to be rounded off into circles whereas true boundaries could not have been circular in all of these countries, but this fuzziness must be due to the lack of sufficient map information from this distant period. The boundaries are much more specific in the map of the Thirty Years Peace 445 BCE image a couple of pages later. The next treaty is from a thousand years later and it concluded the Battle of Qadesh between the Egyptians and the Hittites; it promised "'peace and brotherhood'

for all time", an ambitious goal in any period. One particularly inter-
esting map is of the world in 1 CE as this year is still used as the start
of our yearly calendar. It is historically telling to see the visual of the
giant powers from this period: Roman Empire, Parthian Empire, Han
Empire, and some smaller entities like the Moche and Nazca people in
Southern America. Typically, histories of these individual entities only
show maps of an isolated part of the globe, but many of these places
were trading and otherwise interacting with each other, and such maps
are a great way to show their geographical relationships. These maps
should be helpful if I'm ever writing a history or a fictional work about
the past to catch up on some political highlights from a given period as
well as to check what the geopolitical climate was. Putting all of these
different political entities into a single soup helps to make the world
appear to be a small place with some of the same stories of conquest
and surrender happening in all these different places that propaganda
convinces us are different, but on a giant map that fluidly mutates
over time, they truly become inventions of our imaginations. Do you
know how many states were in the union and who controlled the areas
around them after the Treaty of Paris in 1783 and what did America
ask for of the different neighbors in the dispute? There's a map of this
in this volume.

This is a great source for anybody who needs an encyclopedia of
world history or a set of historic atlases of contested regions across the
world. The grand cover design featuring an image of a meeting between
two disputing leadership delegations and the thick pages and beautiful
color maps also make for a great coffee table book or a book to put on
a shelf as a decoration. Researchers who occasionally mention treaties
form the distant past should find a quick reference to double-check
their memory. Cartographers who study or draw maps will also find
plenty of brand new designs to examine or adopt. This might also be a
great parent for a high school student who might be disoriented about
world history to help put it all into perspective. Highly recommended
for scholars and curious students alike.

ESSAY

IN THE ANTROPOETAS AND MUSES WE TRUST:

READING AND TEACHING THE POETICS ABOUT THE BORDERLANDS AND CHIHUAHUAN DESERT

R. Joseph Rodríguez, California State University, Fresno

Abstract: Using the concept of the *antropoeta* as an ethnographer-observer-poet, the essayist situates the expansive role of cultural and geographic identities and influences of the muses on poets and authors who call the Chihuahuan Desert borderlands as their home. The Chihuahuan Desert covers more than 200,000 square miles, which are mostly situated south of the Río Grande in northern México, although portions lie in Texas, New Mexico, and southeastern Arizona. An emphasis on the expansive Chihuahuan Desert as a source of poetic imagination is also examined to further advance the question of writing where one claims origin and identity.

"What makes the desert beautiful," the little prince said, "is that it hides a well somewhere…"
"Yes," I said to the little prince, "whether it's a house or the stars or the desert, what makes them beautiful is invisible!"
—Antonie de Saint-Exupéry, *The Little Prince* (68)

"We may feel we know what a thing is, but have trouble defining it. That holds as true for poetry as it does for, say, love or electricity."
—Dan Rifenburgh, "What Is Poetry?"

While living in the Southwestern region of the United States, I experienced the borderlands and Chihuahuan Desert as a source of study, teaching, and interpretation via poetry as an inhabitant, educator, and researcher. The poetics of the region and landscape provided new ways of seeing, reading, and rethinking the poetry of the Paso del Norte borderlands and how narratives influence a people's identity formation and affirmation. Even today, students' familiarity with borderlands poets continues to unfold in jagged and established junctures. Nonetheless, students seek to gain more literary fervor as they now study—through close reading and with rigor—the works they seldom encountered in their secondary schooling.

A renewed interest in poetry, bilingualism, and biliteracies, especially in the selected poems that articulate senses of place and home, draw more students into our dialogue for deeper thinking, learning, and questioning as we study a diverse chorus of borderlands poets. Many students in the local schools and universities—and beyond—call on the recovering and rethinking the literary works by U.S.–Mexican and Latinx-origin poets writing the voices and metaphors the borderlands and to incorporate their body of works into our curricula and instruction in both print and digital media formats.

My aim in writing this article, then, is to situate the expansive role of cultural and geographic identities and the influences of the muses in the borderlands with the concept of the *antropoeta*, ethnographer-observer-poet. The emphasis on the expansive Chihuahuan Desert as a source of poetic imagination further advances the question of writing where one claims origin and identity. Specifically, I analyze the poetry that communicates Chihuahuan Desert borderlands narratives, identities, and geographies through language, memory, and form. Frederick Luis Aldama notes, "In today's Latino poetry, we see a smorgasbord of sorts when it comes to ancestry, geographic location, subject matter, and formal device. Nothing is off limits—that is, if we can even speak of limits in the first place" (*Formal* 6).

The poems selected render voice and hope to the borderlands citizens who possess cultural and linguistic wealth. These forms of wealth enrich American poetics and are unlimited and thus create an expansive view toward more global literatures and perspectives. To support the teaching of Latinx poetics, four challenges conceptualized by literacy scholar Ernest Morrell as "practice[s] of powerful English teaching in the 21st century" are incorporated into the discussion to support a pedagogy and dialogue that complements the diverse narratives that constitute American and world literatures (5).

To define Latinx can become a challenge and, for this article, the definition in relation to literatures and identities is best described by Suzanne Bost and Frances R. Aparicio. They remind us:

> The history and politics of US Latino/a literature are distinct. "Latino/a" identity is a product of layers of conquest, colonialism, and cultural mixture—beginning with Western European territorial battles upon indigenous lands of the "New World," from the sixteenth through the nineteenth centuries, and, after most Latin American nations achieved independence, continuing through the US imperialist expansions of the nineteenth century to the present. (2)

This definition interconnected to identities and various influences, from colonization to sociopolitical encounters, inform the article. Last, the following three questions will guide the discussion:

(1) How are the muses influential in the shaping of Latinx poetics, especially for U.S.–Mexican-origin poets in the borderlands?

(2) Do poets write to revise or reframe sanctioned narratives or to incorporate a new vision for the identities, languages, and literacies of desert dwellers? and

(3) What implication, if any, does defining Latinx poetics have for the way we teach and read poetry in our secondary-level schools and university classrooms?

Meeting and Reading the Muses

My earliest memories of the desert and wilderness are hearing stories from the scriptures and later, as an adolescent, while reading poetry written and published by Mexican Americans. From the poets Pat Mora and Benjamin Alire Sáenz, I learned about the Chihuahuan Desert in West Texas and northern México and its influences on desert dwellers, ranging from their everyday lives to their struggles for survival, triumphs as storytellers, and commitment to cultural preservation. Like the desert, their poetry was transformative and offered me sustenance and hope while growing up in a large Latinx community of Houston, Texas. Accordingly, I could dive inward through poetry and also make leaps into worlds so unlike my own, yet interconnected to mine.

While growing up in a large urban area, I oftentimes wanted to explore spaces other than my own to gain experience and understanding—far away from the rules, haunts, and sirens of what seemed a hurried, mundane world I was living in then. Thus, it seemed like my unique calling to find poetry that gave voice and meaning on the page and in the imagination of Mexican and Latinx-origin people living in many parts of Texas, the country, and world. Similar to the prince and pilot in Saint-Exupéry's novella, I sought spaces and writings that "hid a well" (68). The well of poets' imagination became visible with understanding to me as a reader of poetry and later as a teacher and researcher guiding students to read, study, and hear poems closely and slowly—like a poet at work.

Hence, the overflowing wells and reservoirs of energy before me were the Mexican and Latinx-influenced poetics that complemented the classics I was assigned to read as a high school and university student. I learned what the essential canon works were in my public schooling and university studies. Any other works were remained overlooked, unspoken, and unknown. Either way, a young reader like me could have interpreted this slight as a message that the poetics reflecting my world mattered little in my teachers' development of curricula and planning of instruction. As a result, I memorized and saluted the canonical myths, gods, and goddesses I was required to read and revere in my public schooling and in some of my undergraduate courses. I wanted to possess literary rigor and acumen. Conversely, I became drawn to stories that could relate to the lives absent in the assigned readings, but that I could possibly complement with my own reading goals outside of my public schooling and university studies.

In fact, I became drawn to the lesser-read myths and overlooked arts from ancient Greece and Mesopotamia. I wanted to know which additional narratives and perspectives existed and were not included in school readers and university anthologies. The works and pages not often revered as "literature" or "American" were skipped and, when pursued further, a few teachers and professors shared, in confidence, that they were unfamiliar and thus uncomfortable teaching any literary works new to them. I followed their lessons and syllabi nevertheless, and I succeeded in my course work. The indifference to recovered and revisionist literature was, at best, ignored, and it resembled then and even now patterns of colonization and marginalization that directly influence what students experience as readers to opportunities to gain literacies for democracy and self-affirmation. Aldama observes,

> The different histories of migration and policies toward Latinos (or of borders moving over populations as in the case of those living in the northern Mexican territories known today as the Southwest) have led to different experiences with access to education and literacy. The use of English (and less and less Spanish) by Latino/a authors is largely socioeconomically and historically determined. (*Latino/a* 4)

Still, I wondered how a more pluralistic vision of American and world literatures could be realized and taught. Admittedly, I valued the classical literatures I was told mattered most for surviving the test of time, instruction, and assessment but with some skepticism. In the critical essay "Unspeakable Things Unspoken: The Afro-American presence American Literature," Toni Morrison concedes, "Canon building is empire building. Canon defense is national defense" (8). In the reading program I developed as my own diverse empire to become learned, I began to pay more attention to the roles of the nine daughters of Zeus and Mnemosyne, who are recognized as the Muses of knowledge and the arts, and competing voices to the master narrative too often upheld as the only story about our civilization.

In *The Raft of Odysseus: The Ethnographic Imagination of Homer's Odyssey*, Carol Dougherty believes, "The poet [Homer] respectfully identifies himself as merely mortal in comparison with the Muses—they know all; he knows nothing—and then proceeds to produce poetry that sets the standard against which all future poets will measure themselves" (24). The Muses are summoned in epic poetry and other narratives for inspiration, guidance, and help by many adventurers and explorers. Reliance upon them can yield to escape and triumph in the face of hardship, tumult, and hopelessness.

Similarly, in Mexican and U.S.–México borderlands literatures, I learned that many poets often call on "*La décima musa de América*" for affirmation and vision, and she offers guidance toward an epiphany or catharsis. The Tenth Muse of the hemispheric Américas is Sor Juana Inés de la Cruz, the seventeenth-century scholar, nun, and poet from San Miguel de Nepantla, México. Sor Juana is revered as an inspiration to many Chicanx and Latinx poets who seek her interceding in their life of letters and quest as witnesses. To illustrate, in a recent critical book titled *[Un]Framing the "Bad Woman" Sor Juana, Malinche, Coyolxauhqui, and Other Rebels with a Cause*, Alicia Gaspar de Alba acknowledges, "For the past five years, I have been living with Sor Juana in my head, my heart, and my dreams. I have been researching her life, listening to the underside of her words, letting her entrap and guide me through the webs of logic, pun, and metaphor that she so meticulously spun in her writing" (41).

Gaspar de Alba's reflective meditation and scholarly research reveals many ways that we can rethink and reframe the stories and poetics about women and societies across history, time, and systems. She repositions the rebels that been dismissed in history and gives voice to their points of view with primary and secondary sources. Counternarratives and diverse points of view create the possibilities of finally telling a larger, more complex story that merits our attention and instruction as educators and readers of poetry. This is the case about the poetics from the borderlands and Chihuahuan Desert in the effort to challenge colonialism and indifference that persists about native cultures, peoples, and languages. Instead, poetics can provide a sense of origin and place for a people seeking to understand and experience the meanings through languages and a sense of place in their homelands.

Literature can affirm and redeem a people and country dispossessed from literary history and canons. In the essay "What Is Poetry?," Dan Rifenburgh explains,

> Like other forms of literature, poetry may seek to tell a story, enact a drama, convey ideas, offer vivid, unique description or express our inward spiritual, emotional, or psychological states. Yet, poetry pays particular close attention to words themselves: their sounds, textures, patterns, and meanings. It takes special pleasure in focusing on the verbal music inherent in language.

The literary elements of poetry described by Rifenburgh encapsulate the varied possibilities that a poem can deliver and articulate for both speakers and readers of poems.

Along the same lines of Sor Juana as a revered visionary, we can find reservoirs of inspiration, energy, and hope from many poets for a writing life. Mine have been poets and thinkers who write about the borderlands and desert—at the turn of the century to today. Situated in what has become one of the longest borders of enforcement in the world, the Chihuahuan Desert is the largest desert in North America. It covers more than 200,000 square miles, which are mostly situated south of the Río Grande in northern México, although portions lie in Texas, New Mexico, and southeastern Arizona. This vast desert and space offers many perspectives in poetry that reveal the geographies of domination, imperialism, power, and linguistic oppression, which are not foreign here nor to the greater hemispheric Américas.

The desert can be easily overlooked as barren and dry, yet in its vastness so much is concealed and revealed here to native people and newly transplanted neighbors. In its varied state, the desert can be just as giving and resilient for human, animal, and plant life. Mora observes, "Th[is] desert—its firmness, resilience, and its fierceness, its whispered chants and tempestuous dance, its wisdom and majesty—shape[s] us as geography always shapes its inhabitants" (*Nepantla* 13). The shaping of both identities and geographies can merge through poetry as we examine selected poetry in this article.

Antropoetas

Poetry invites readers to make connections across time, experiences, and cultures and to become present through language and form by making the poem part of this moment, *now*. Jane Hirshfield emphasizes, "Poetry's work is not simply the recording of inner and outer perception; it makes by words and music new possibilities of perceiving. [...] A work of art is not a piece of fruit lifted from a tree branch: it is a ripening collaboration of artist, receiver, and world" (3-4). Also, poetry can transform and fuel our imagination and soul as we gain understanding and elaborate the poem's conversation alongside our living experience. In all forms, poetry reminds us to be present and awake: human and humane. As such, a chorus of Chicanx and Latinxpoetics reveals how their voices tell the story of place and memory through what Renato Rosaldo names as "*antropoesía*," or ethnographic poetics (106). Much like the role and craft of "poet as *curandera*" that Mora urges us to consider for the Chicana writer, Rosaldo provides a complementary lens that invites a balance of the senses and deep inquiry (*Nepantla* 127). The antropoeta approach is driven by mindfulness and self-reflection to gain deeper meaning and understanding—as jagged or "uneven" as it may be, in the shaping of observation and poems for readers.

Rosaldo and Mora's vision of a poet's craft and contribution are both instructive and affirming for me as an educator and writer. Theirs is a meditative, reflective labor that can be fulfilling for the poet and reader through concentrated use of language and our senses. In fact, Rosaldo elaborates the work of the *antropoeta* much further in the effort to make sense and meaning from the world and interconnected relationships:

> Like an ethnographer, the antropoeta looks and looks, listens and listens, until she [sic] sees or hears what she did not apprehend at first. This form of inquiry resembles field research in that it involves observation, asking questions, attending with patience and care, knowing that meaning may be there, waiting to be found, even if the observer-poet does not yet know what it is.... My task, as a poet, is to render intelligible what is complex and to bring home to the reader the uneven and contradictory shape of that moment. (107)

An example of the poet as *curandera* and *antropoeta* can be found in various narratives of the borderlands. As an illustration, in Mora's poem "Bribe," the speaker invokes and persuades the desert through a ceremonial incantation to gain the gift of voice and imagination for her craft. Although the modern meaning of the word "bribe" is a gift used to influence or persuade someone to do something unethical, Mora uses the term as a positive connotation. In the poem, the word "bribe" means to make an offering or sacrifice accompanied by a call or prayer for Mother Earth's help and interceding. The word "bribe" comes from an early French word meaning "a morsel of bread given to beggars," but today it has a negative connotation.

The speaker in the poem observes Native American women celebrating and honoring the earth and natural world in voice, song, and ceremony. The traditions of American Indians, Mexicans, and Mexican Americans are present in the opening stanza that reads:

I hear Indian women
 chanting, chanting
I see them long ago bribing
the desert with turquoise threads,
in the silent morning coolness,
kneeling, digging, burying
their offering in the Land
 chanting, chanting
   Guide my hands, Mother,
   to weave singing birds
   flowers rocking in the wind, to trap
   them on my cloth with a web of thin threads.
(*My Own True Name* 57)

Earth is personified as "Mother" and from whom Native American women request guidance. Moreover, there is a comparison to spiders weaving a web, which recalls indigenous people's myths about Spider Grandmother. Acts of "kneeling, digging, [and] burying" confirm the human journey as sacred and one with the earth as turquoise threads are offered as a "bribe" to the land. The speaker identifies with indigenous women and the Chihuahuan Desert as she summons her muses as a poet.

As the poem unfolds, the speaker, who may possibly be Mora herself, then calls on the Chihuahuan Desert, her muse, for inspiration and to fuel her writing life. The speaker seeks to barter with her instruments to meet nature in the second and final stanza:

Secretly I scratch a hole in the desert
by my home. I bury a ballpoint pen
and lined yellow paper. Like the Indians
I ask the Land to smile on me, to croon
softly, to help me catch her music with words. (*My Own True Name* 57)

In a reversal of roles from observer to actor, the speaker in the poem seeks to develop her craft and to honor not only traditions, but also the beauty found in nature with affirmations through language that is transformed into poetry. Like the indigenous women, the speaker offers a "bribe" to the "Land" as well, except hers is a ballpoint pen and paper. Together, the women's offerings suit their craft, which is weaving, while the speaker's craft is writing.

As women weave pictures of the natural world, the speaker wants to write about nature; they complement each other as translators of the beauty of the natural world into designs and words. Overall, the speaker's diverse identities and connections are significant to begin her poetic narrative that is one with culture and nature and affirms mestizo identities with the meeting of indigenous and Mexican-Spanish civilizations and heritages.

To Observe

"Writers are observers," explains Amitava Kumar (xiii). In observation like the *antropoeta*, the poet awakens language with the possibilities of testimonies that witness earth and humans coming alive about their senses of identity and origin as well as departures. Through sensual imagery of river water, as noted in Joseph Delgado's poem titled "dirty," survival and resilience accompany the speaker to make meaning and a life:

> 4.
> on the river I could smell the waters
>   thick at my nose,
>   scurrying across my chest,
>   war beaten
>   forest of salt-cedar
>   forest of dark leaves,
> like an ageless dust come
> hunting my bones over hills
>   and deserts
> and mountains of stone. (4)

The spacing of the poem communicates the flow of water as well as the jagged sense of being the speaker experiences in the wholesomeness of nature, a revelatory muse.

For Saenz, the desert is fiercely majestic as revealed so meticulously in the poem "Meditation on Living in the Desert, No. 1." In just three lines, the speaker reveals the ordinary and extraordinary power of his muse, the desert world, through a form of a ritual, communion, and affirmation:

The rains do not always come.
The winds remain.

The dust will gather on your tongue. (*The Book of What Remains* 5)

Moreover, the desert can be just as relenting and giving to the speaker in a faithful and spiritual journey as witnessed in the poem "To the Desert" by Saenz. In the poem, the speaker who possesses *antropoeta* acumen with the desert as both muse and giver:

I came to you one rainless August night.
You taught me how to live without the rain.
You are thirst and thirst is all I know.

. .   .   .

You wrap your name tight around my ribs
And keep me warm. I was born for you.
Above, below, by you, by you surrounded.
I wake to you at dawn. Never break your
Knot. Reach, rise, blow, *Sálvame, mi dios,*
Trágame, mi tierra. Salva, traga, Break me,
I am bread. I will be the water for your thirst. (*Dark and Perfect Angels* 96)

The physical and spiritual needs are revealed in the poem as the speaker follows a journey that possesses an omnipresence larger than the self. The speaker and desert barter in many ways like in Mora's poem "Bribe" to become full and whole again.

In the poem "Bones" by Sheryl Luna, the speaker establishes a sense of place for readers as we enter the borderlands with a concept of origin, the realism of what transpires and dies, and what is remembered through vivid memory and once-spoken languages as if for an *antropoeta*. The deliberate actions of humans reveal memories, losses, and gains:

And I remember that it is good to be born of dust,
born amid cardboard shanties of sweet gloom.
I remember that the bare cemetery stones
in El Paso and Juárez hold the music, and each spring
when the winds carry the dust of loss there is a howl,
a surge of something unbelievable, like death,
like the collapse of language, like the frail bones
of Mexican grandmothers singing. (*Pity the Drowned Horses* 3-4)

Although titled "Bones," the poem renders a new interpretation of
bones as the title and even redefines the word for readers as if it were
a Georgia O'Keefe canvas on display through a poem. Moreover, the
poem ends with "Mexican grandmothers singing" in affirmation for
many lives lived and similar to the speaker in Mora's poem "Bribe" and
from whom we hear "chanting" in the continuous present tense.

In a deep observation through the speaker who is a gas station clerk,
we gain insights about human labor and violence through various situ-
ations in Luna's poem "Lowering Your Standards for Food Stamps,"
which is included in its entirety here.

Words fall out of my coat pocket,
soak in bleach water. I touch everyone's
dirty dollars. Maslow's got everything on me.
Fourteen hours on my feet. No breaks.
No smokes or lunch. Blank-eyed movements:
trash bags, coffee burner, fingers numb.
I am hourly protestations and false smiles.
The clock clicks its slow slowing.
Faces blur in a stream of hurried soccer games,
sunlight, and church certainty. I have no
poem to carry, no material illusions.
Cola spilled on hands, so sticky fingered,
I'm far from poems. I'd write of politicians,
refineries, and a border's barbed wire,
but I am unlearning America's languages
with a mop. In a summer-hot red
polyester top, I sell lotto tickets. Cars wait for gas
billowing black. Killing time has new meaning.
A jackhammer breaks apart a life. The slow globe

spirals, and at night black space has me dizzy.
Visionaries off their meds and wacked out
meth heads sing to me. A panicky fear of robbery
and humiliation drips with my sweat.
Words some say are weeping twilight and sunrise.
I am drawn to dramas, the couple arguing, the man
headbutting his wife in the parking lot.
911: no metered aubade, and nobody but

myself to blame.

The title, both fitting as a paradox and oxymoron, is dissected in a line-by-line approach to reveal the speaker's witnessing of American labor and life. The bigger questions about public assistance are turned upside-down as we learn that the public needs not only assistance to live and co-exist for essentials, but assistance to survive through violence enacted upon fellow humans.

With irony and several literary devices, Luna delivers the shame and scam of public assistance that dehumanizes those who are attempting to live and thrive. The public's interpretation of advancement and progress are placed at the forefront for two audiences: the speaker who faces American life and American dreams and the reader who is both vicarious observer and also trying to make ends meet. The reader learns about the mundane existences and even movements of a modern world. In essence, the world the speaker inhabits and participates in daily can easily become indifferent and inhumane as well as detached as one "unlearn[s] America's languages" as opportunity keeps taking different form and possibility erasure if it ever existed for the majority of Americans. The speaker fulfills the role of an antropoeta, as does Luna, as witness in struggle.

In the poem "The Towers" by Rafael Jesús González, the speaker remembers September 11, 2001, and places the Twin Towers in relation to other towers across time and sacred texts. Within the poem, humanity is challenged against injustice and revenge. Instead, the speaker imagines a world created by humans who pledge for the common good in a world filled with chaos and injury. The speaker favors justices and exhorts the just.

(September 11, 2001)

The towers fall as if,
seen through crossed eyes,
a Goliath fell brought down by a David.

Behind the myths
who of us is the guilty?
Who the innocent?
What is the distance
between justice and vengeance?

Death is inevitable, not fair.
And when the innocent are caught
in the webs of violence, it is terrible.

May the Earth hold them in rest.
If we would make a monument
worthy of their deaths,
in honor & memory of them,
let us pledge ourselves
to freedom,
true justice,
world peace.

For if death be not just
let just be our lives.

The poem appears in a Spanish-language version by González and
as "Las Torres":

(11 septiembre 2001)

Se derriban las torres como
si visto por ojos cruzados,
cayera un Goliat abatido por un David.

Detrás de los mitos
¿quiénes somos los culpables?
¿quiénes los inocentes?
¿Cual es la distancia
entre la justicia y la venganza?

La muerte es inevitable, no justa.
Y cuando los inocentes caen
en las redes de la violencia, es terrible.

Que la Tierra los tenga en descanso.
Si monumento hiciéramos
digno de sus muertes
en honor y memoria de ellos
comprometámonos
a la libertad,
a la justicia verdadera,
a la paz mundial.

Que si la muerte no es justa,
justas sean nuestras vidas.

The speaker's observation, perception, and interpretation favor an imagined world filled with justice and where the meek can prevail. In short, a self-pledge and a worldly pledge for the common good and necessary justice must prevail.

The concept of *antropoeta* appears in many poems about the borderlands, especially when the speaker appears in a first-person point of view. The *antropoeta*-speaker attempts to name and redefine identities and spaces that remained unnamed in literature for centuries, relegated to the margin, in complete absence in public and print life, and erased from dialogue and conversation in histories and literatures distributed for reading and instruction in borderlands public and private education. Overall, borderlands poetry can engage diverse perspectives through identities and narratives that elicit deeper questioning and thinking.

Counternarratives versus the Single Story

Whose stories matter? Whose story becomes poetry and canonical for study? The telling of stories varies from chronicler to historian. This holds true in the diverse voices of poetry from the borderlands. It can be instructive to learn from Ricardo Castro-Salazar and Carl Bagley about the main narrative that appears in history and literature. They explain, "The Master Narrative acts like a powerful filter that tells us that the U.S. has been built by [W]hite European settlers and that the founding civilization of this country was Anglo-Protestant. Thus, non-English speakers, brown, black and yellow people are seen as strangers, aliens, and 'others'" (8). The filter they describe reveals the "danger of a single story" as Chimamanda Ngozi Adichie explains in a TED Talk. As a result, counternarratives, or stories in opposition to the "Master Narrative," advance multiple viewpoints.

Castro-Salazar and Bagley note that those who are too often absent, erased, or misrepresented "create counter-histories in order to incorporate their own experience into the national narrative. These counter-histories, however, do not claim to be the definite history. Definite stories do not exist; different accounts of events nurture our histories and identities. (Perhaps that is why "history" and "story" are the same word in Spanish [*historia*])" (8). The counternarrative is present via poetic forms in Latinx poetry and borderlands poetry in the effort to recover literary history that includes witnesses and testimonies. World languages such as Spanish and indigenous languages provide lenses into narratives often untold, but are now being articulated via poetry and other genres.

The concept of the *antropoeta* and "poet as *curandera*" articulate the role of the poet as a storyteller, listener, and skilled griot who tells the *historias* in need of telling, reading, and performance. The storyteller may be from the colonial era to the present. For instance, in the multi-narrative titled *Counternarratives: Stories and Novellas*, Keene's narrative places into perspective the role of the Roman Catholic Church with native people as he writes, "The clergy had one method dealing with the Indians, soldier another. The Colonel, no Jesuit, urged his men to pursue the last of the savages until they were incapable of staging even the memory of a surprise. There were therefore no natives who could be pressed into serving as guides" (p. 11). The methods noted in Keene's storytelling technique are just as applicable and relevant to the counternarrative methods adopted in Latinx poetry and borderlands poetry.

To maintain and advance the presence of the *antropoeta*, John Alba Cutler insists, "Chicano/a literary works celebrate Chicano/a culture, which has been devalued and denigrated in the United States, yet these same works know that attempts to represent that culture inevitably transform it. [...] Chicano/a literature, by virtue of its literariness, pinpoints serious blindspots in assimilation sociology" (11). The assimilationist narrative is challenged by borderlands poets through both acculturation and creative narratives that reveal multi-literacies through testimony and witnessing of struggle and triumph. Specifically, in Andrea Blancas Beltran's poem "Reading and Writing Lessons," the speaker Beltran reveals the meaning of literacies, for whom literacies are accessible, and how literacies are enacted. Beltran's first stanza reads:

> I remember the day I learned
> about my grandmother teaching
> herself to read and write. I was being nosy
> in her living room cabinets and found
> her workbooks, similar to the ones I took to school,
> cassette tapes, too. Back then,
> I thought literacy was free and that everyone
> took advantage. She signed cards only when holidays
> and birthdays demanded and wrote the occasional shopping list.

Beltran's poem incorporates the challenges faced by students who once sought knowledge, schooling, and education. The speaker describes herself as "nosy" as she becomes *antropoeta* in her grandmother's house and comes to understand her self-education to become literate and participatory. The poem hints at education history and periods in which resources were scarce, and some books and media were shared across grade levels and age groups to become learned and to participate in society. As revealed in the full poem, borderlands citizens' efforts were hindered, since schooling in native, borderlands languages were absent as well as across the greater United States.

Despite generational differences as well as historical, social, and political realities affecting access to a literate life between a grandmother and her granddaughter in the poem, they share the pursuit of knowledge and to make meaning happen as they communicate and bond across time, limitations, resources, and events. The poem functions as a counternarrative by communicating how literacy is enacted for engagement and how the speaker relies on literacy for existence despite the limited access to schooling and education she once experienced. Through literacy, the grandmother and granddaughter communicate, exist, and affirm their origins, identities, and mutual love.

Public monuments and spaces advance narratives that are often in opposition to the local people's sense of place and history. To take a case in point and in response to a tourist-friendly narrative I found on May 2nd, 2015, while visiting the Wyler Aerial Tramway State Park, I wrote the following poem and subtitled it "Variation on a Theme by Lucille Clifton."

at Sierra de los Mansos, 2nd May 2015
Wyler Aerial Tramway State Park

nobody says the names
the given names by first peoples
to rocks once moved so moved
by the people calling this home
now unidentified and indistinct
instead we only hear of purchases
and treasures galore of land
the ranger remembers with glories
claimed yet he does not know
the names we know of the sacred
rocks and hands once touching earth
some bodies sat here and carved
mountains of lineage with rocks
fed fish and manna on these rocks
how waters once flooded the land
shaping rocks and adobe we behold
before us as we ascend into the sky
and rock bed flowers bloom
we know the rocks must know
their own deserted names
and our ancestral names
even if we misremember
or forget to ask what pages
were rewritten without us
without telling what was
and is native and holy here
somebody manifested another
telling by making one history

after the coming of franklin in 1848
erasing some memories and names
we remember and pronounce

El Paso del Norte, Tejas, USA
Chihuahuan Desert

The poem serves as a counternarrative and testimony of additional histories that surround a natural space—a mountain—by one of the First Peoples, the Mansos, who honored the sacred and meanings of the mountain to both humans and Mother Earth. Admittedly, the power of naming and the removal of names communicates the telling of one dominant and exclusive narrative through the erasure of native people in public spaces. Regardless, the people's sense of memory maintains alive the relevant narratives and in response to colonization and disregard in the written documentation advanced by the state.

The counternarrative also serves as a response to borderlands chaos, terror, and violence that citizens face in their everyday life. Despite El Paso's designation as one of the safest cities in the United States and with reduced crime and violence in the neighboring Ciudad Juárez, Chihuahua, México, the media narratives are neither neatly delineated nor easily categorized for consumption by citizens in both cities. For example, in the poem "Mexadus" by Jorge A. Gómez, the reader enters the poem *in medias res* as images unfold with hardship, abandonment, and flight. In the first two stanzas, we witness a people seeking to be delivered from violence, terror, and crime to make a promised life in the borderlands.

The structure and design of Gómez's poem "Mexadus" resembles the jagged lives endured by borderlands citizens and functions as a book, or poem, of the continental Mexican people's exodus and possibly their diaspora between native territories. Consider the first two stanzas in which the speaker serves as *antropoeta* and eyewitness of a war zone in actual time as the reader moves from line to line with a feeling of brokenness. Here violence is enacted upon the innocent who are neither protected nor guilty:

call it
the Mexadus,
miles
en fuga,
pavimentos 'turrados in metal
shells,
yellow tabs beneath
a bulletholed
Escape.

calcined corpses
divested faces
decorate deserts,
cartels crucify
cadavers to trees
of carbon age
zapotecas revere,
Zetas toss
Molotovs,
bottled
mercurochrome
combusts in
farmacias.

Gómez's poem's title mirrors the linguistic innovation of border-lands languaging and poetic sensibility of the *antropoeta* as language-maker. Moreover, the poem provides various scenes and sequences of history and violence that include México's indigenous people as well as bodies unaccounted in the Chihuahuan Desert, yet noted through the everyday assassinations and violence in the making. The word "Escape" appears in its own line as an imperative, which is an apt arrangement and command in the poem. Overall, Escape becomes synonymous with Mexadus and as a fit description. The borderlands citizens' most promising opportunity is to flee for their lives and livelihood. The Mexadus in progress reveals the incendiary circumstances within a drug and crime warfare state.

The poetry volume *The Verging Cities* by Natalie Scenters-Zapico is a model of the counternarrative in response to the single story consumed by the general public. In the poem "How Borders Are Built," the speaker describes from a bedroom how she loses her own self, body, and agency in the authority and hands of others through an enactment that is cyclical, numbing, and violent:

> You lay on blue sheets. I put two fingers in my mouth and they disappear.
> In your hair a crown of border patrol point their guns at me; they watch
> with night vision goggles to see if I'll wade across our river. I lick
>
> the black corners of your ears; one agent shoots my shoulder. I wonder if you
> could take them down while you're on top of me, put them in a box somewhere.
> I tell you I am desert: my face cracks; reptiles hide in my shadows[.]
> .   .   .   .
> [...] We eat our border every hundred years then build it up again. We ask each other if we've carried any foreign items today, barbed wire
> fences stapled to our teeth, avocado pits in our back pocket. We say no. (4)

The speaker communicates how violent acts toward one's body have similarities with those enacted by border law enforcement. Consumption and decomposition of the body appear in nature's presence, even as humans attempt to comply with authority and coexist with nature. At the same time, the building of borders occurs across centuries and to the detriment, and even demise, of borderlands citizens.

In Scenters-Zapico's poem "The Verging Cities Watch Me," two cities are transformed as possessing omniscience and vision through human connections. The speaker takes our hand and walks us through the streets of her hometown to a scenic area that can be considered romantic. However, reality soon dominates the vision of what two cities are as well as crime scenes too familiar to escape from one's own body and aloneness as a witness:

> I walk home from a bar alone, stop
>   on Rim Road to let the lights of El Paso
>   and Ciudad Juárez switch on

and off, sew themselves over all the ugly
    of my body. I hold my breath and hope
all that light will turn

into black beetles to swarm me quiet.
    But when I open my body I am alone,
        alone only the way these two cities can be

        alone, only the way I am alone with him.
    When we are naked, we are pale as fliers
for women gone missing. (19)

The cities are personified as feeling aloneness, while the speaker's body and her lover's are no different from the disappeared women of the twin cities now verging in narrative poetry and human plight.

History and poetry are interrelated in the making of the counternarrative to function as a text that is in response to a "Master Narrative" that dominated and was sanctioned as the official text and narrative. Furthermore, the function of the counternarrative in borderlands poetry is best summed up by Ricardo Castro-Salazar and Carl Bagley as they define history which is relevant, and possibly synonymous, with poetry. They add:

> History is not what occurred in the past, but merely a story of what people thought and experienced at the time an event occurred. Inevitably, the belief system and context of the narrator (the historian or individual recalling the past) influence any interpretation, modern or otherwise. Thus, historical narratives are continually retold and elucidated, undergoing vast transformation as they are reinterpreted at different points in time. (p. 4)

The poems presented as counternarratives fulfill the promise of revisiting, revising, and rethinking histories we deemed accurate or even as the sole pre-interpreted account that must remain unchallenged and untouched. Instead, borderlands poets reframe the essential questions and sanctioned narratives via *antropoeta* and "poet as *curandera*" to examine interpretations across time and space.

Four Challenges for Reading and Teaching

In the essay "Teaching English POWERFULLY: Four Challenges," Ernest Morrell insists, "No matter what technological innovations arise, the core classroom transactions are between teachers and students, students and students, and students and the texts they consume and create" (5). Similar to the antropoeta, we can teach out students close reading and critical thinking strategies to read poetry like a poet and in society for action and change. Most specifically, the relationships that we build with students to advance the reading of poetry must be led by the four challenges Morrell proposes for our instructional planning and learning connections:

Challenge #1: Develop powerful readers of multicultural texts.
Challenge #2: Develop powerful authors of multimodal texts.
Challenge #3: Connect classroom production to social action.
Challenge #4: Connect the discipline around the student.

The four challenges were used within this text to advance the reading of poetry through the lenses of an *antropoeta* in the presence of muses influencing identities and cultures of the borderlands and Chihuahuan Desert.

In support of these four challenges, one recent achievement and influence connected to the power of world languages and poetry is Juan Felipe Herrera. In June 2015, Herrera was named the 51st Poet Laureate at the Library of Congress for 2015–2017. In his work and laureateship, Herrera sought to advance the work of poetry across economics, politics, and society. For Herrera, the chaos and challenges of the world are not absent in his poetics.

For example, in the poem titled "Ayotzinapa," Herrera memorializes a group of teachers who went missing, from the Ayotzinapa Normal School near Iguala, Guerrero, México. His poems is a remembrance of their lives and actions.

From Ayotzinapa we were headed toward Iguala to say to the
mayor that we wanted funds for our rural school for teachers

no one knew it no one saw it
    we are learning this number   43 for you
        because there were   43 of us

we are
not disposable
9-26-14   (17)

Poetry, including borderlands poetry, must remain connected to the everyday world and struggle for justice and freedom.

On September 16, 2015, Herrera presented his inaugural reading at the Library of Congress in Washington, DC. "When we say poetry, it's really the vision of all voices," Herrera explained. "It's freedom. [...] When you use your own voice, freely, then we're all united." Herrera's new poem titled "Imagine What You Could Do" and the recording from the event capture his earliest memories of speaking Spanish and struggling to learn and speak English while a student in elementary school. The poem vibrates with energy, resilience, and the vision to become a U.S. poet laureate. The final stanza reads:

If I stood up
wearing a robe
in front of my familia and many more
on the high steps
of the Library of Congress
in Washington, D.C., and read
out loud and signed
my poetry book
like this—
'poet laureate of the United States of
America'
Imagine what you could do.

As teachers, we can understand these feelings within our students, within ourselves, and given voice in poetry. We can encourage our students and colleagues to reach their highest potential, too.

Herrera's third-grade teacher, Leyla Sampson, encouraged the young Herrera as an emerging reader, singer, and writer in her classroom in the 1950s. Early on, Herrera exhibited a fondness for words and languages. He recalls singing "Three Blind Mice" as Ms. Sampson listened intently. Her assessment confirmed his resilience: "You have a beautiful voice." (Here, assessment is used in the sense of the Latin word *assidere*, which means "to sit beside.")

On Herrera's inaugural reading night, guess who sat in the audience? Ms. Sampson! Indeed, the attentive listener, sitting patiently before her student again, was Leyla Sampson, who is now ninety-four years old. Herrera, who is sixty-six years old, shared with Ms. Sampson and his audience, "It was your words that made it all happen for me.

All poetry is influenced by world languages, literatures, and cultures. Thus, as educators and readers, the challenges are significant for our teaching and reading lives. Through deliberate planning, we can welcome more readers to poetry waiting to be read and sung by children, adolescents, and adult alike.

Trusting Muses and Poems at the Table

In the United States, from September 15th through October 15th, we observe National Hispanic Heritage Month. This period marks the celebration of diverse cultures, histories, and contributions of Americans whose ancestors came from various lands with changing frontiers and borderlands across time and space: Spain, México, the Caribbean, and Central and South America.

Our classrooms are filled with opportunities to advance the contributions of Hispanic and Latinx Americans from the literary, performance, and visual arts to scientific research. The continental Américas, as a hemispheric whole, is rich with generations of heritages interconnected with Latino life and thought and include indigenous people's influences and contributions. Through language, poets make the natural world and our senses visible and to experience with reflection and memory. Poetry and memory can be joined in communion as we witness, document, and teach poetry as *antropoetas*. The borderlands poetry that exhibits linguistic innovation can be savored by more readers who are guests at a literary banquet when we offer invitation and places at the table for many cultures, identities, muses, and poems. Our openness to experience and understanding can create a movement about how poetry ignites our lives with meaning and hope. We can open more doors and windows to poetry and world languages at our table.

The poets and thinkers included in this article merit reading in their entirety, because their poems beckon us as readers, writers, thinkers, and performers to their craft, muses, and vision. As readers and teachers of poetry, we are committed to the spoken, celebrated word. In fact, the poems we welcome to our conversations and classrooms—including those that our students and colleagues have penned, texted, typed, or just Tweeted—must remind us and our students about the mutual and reciprocal relationships that poetry can feed and fuel in our everyday lives and across literary tables within and beyond the borderlands and Chihuahuan Desert.

Works Cited

Adichie, Chimamanda Ngozi. "The Danger of a Single Story." *TED-Talks*, July 2009, https://www.ted.com/talks/chimamanda_adichie_the_danger_of_a_single_story. Accessed 20 Aug. 2018.

Aldama, Frederick Luis. *Formal Matters in Contemporary Latino Poetry.* Palgrave Macmillan, 2013.

—. "Introduction." *Latino/a Literature in the Classroom: Twenty-First Century Approaches to Teaching*, edited by Frederick Luis Aldama, Routledge, 2015, pp. 1-10.

Beltran, Andrea Blancas. "Reading and Writing Lessons." *Acentos Review*, Feb. 2013, http://www.andreabeltran.com/work/. Accessed 1 Aug. 2018.

Bebout, Lee. "Postracial Mestizaje: Richard Rodriguez's Racial Imagination in an America Where Everyone Is Beginning to Melt." *American Studies*, vol. 54, no. 1, 2015, pp. 89-113.

Bost, Suzanne, and Frances R. Aparicio. "Introduction." *The Routledge Companion to Latino/a Literature*, edited by Suzanne Bost and Frances R. Aparicio, Routledge, 2014, pp. 1-10.

Castro-Salazar, Ricardo, and Carl Bagley. *Navigating Borders: Critical Race Theory Research and Counter History of Undocumented Americans.* Peter Lang Publishing, 2012.

Cisneros, Sandra. *A House of My Own: Stories from My Life.* Knopf, 2015.

Cutler, John Alba. *Ends of Assimilation: The Formation of Chicano Lit-*

erature. Oxford UP, 2015.

Delgado, Joseph. *Ditch Water: Poems.* Kórima P, 2013.

Dougherty, Carol. *The Raft of Odysseus: The Ethnographic Imagination of Homer's Odyssey.* Oxford UP, 2001.

Gaspar de Alba, Alicia. *[Un]Framing the "Bad Woman": Sor Juana, Malinche, Coyolxauhqui, and Other Rebels with a Cause.* University of Texas P, 2014.

Gomez, Jorge A. "Mexadus." *Acentos Review,* May 2013, http://www.acentosreview.com/May_2013/Gomez.html. Accessed 1 July 2018.

González, Rafael Jesús. "Las Torres." *Abalone Moon: A Journal of Poetry and the Arts.* Fall 2007, http://www.abalonemoon.com/fall/gonzalez.html. Accessed 1 Aug. 2018.

González, Rafael Jesús. "The Towers." *Abalone Moon: A Journal of Poetry and the Arts.* Fall 2007, http://www.abalonemoon.com/fall/gonzalez.html. Accessed 5 Aug. 2018.

Herrera, Juan Felipe. *Notes on the Assemblage.* City Lights Books, 2015.

Hirshfield, Jane. *Ten Windows: How Great Poems Transform the World.* Knopf, 2015.

Intrator, Sam M., and Megan Scribner, editors. *Teaching with Heart: Poetry That Speaks to the Courage to Teach.* Jossey-Bass, Wiley, 2014.

Keene, John. *Counternarratives: Stories and Novellas.* New Directions Publishing, 2015.

Kumar, Amitava. *Lunch with a Bigot: The Writer in the World.* Duke UP, 2015.

Leen, Catherine, and Niamh Thornton, editors. *International Perspectives on Chicana/o Studies: "This World is My Place."* Routledge, 2013.

Luna, Sheryl. "Lowering Your Standards for Food Stamps." *Poetry,* vol. 204, no. 1, 2014, p. 29.

—. *Pity the Drowned Horses.* University of Notre Dame P, 2005.

—. *Seven.* A Taos P, 2013.

—. "Shock and Awe." *Poetry,* vol. 204, no. 1, 2014, p. 28.

Martínez, Pablo Miguel. *Brazos, Carry Me: Poems.* Kórima P, 2013.

Martín-Junquera, Imelda, ed. *Landscapes of Writing in Chicano Literature.* Palgrave Macmillan, 2013.

Mora, Pat. *Adobe Odes.* U of Arizona P, 2006.

—. *Chants.* Arte Público P, 1985.

—. *My Own True Name: New and Selected Poems for Young Adults, 1984–1999.* Arte   Público P, Piñata Books, 2000.

—. *Nepantla: Essays from the Land in the Middle.* U of New Mexico P, 2008.

Morrell, Ernest. "Teaching English POWERFULLY: Four Challenges." *English in Texas: A Journal of the Texas Council of Teachers of English Language Arts*, vol. 45, no. 1, 2015, pp. 5-7.

Morrison, Toni. "Unspeakable Things Unspoken: The Afro-American Presence American Literature." *Michigan Quarterly Review*, vol. 28, no. 1, 1989, pp. 1-34.

Nelson, Chad M. "Resisting Whiteness: Mexican American Studies and Rhetorical Struggles for Visibility." *Journal of International and Intercultural Communication*, vol. 8, no. 1, 2015, pp. 63-80.

Pentecost, Rose Anna. "Indigenous and Spanish Transculturation: Becoming Mexican American." *Plaza: Dialogues in Language and Literature*, vol. 5, no. 1, Winter 2014, pp.   39-47.

Rana, Swati. "Reading Brownness: Richard Rodriguez, Race, and Form." *American Literary   History*, vol. 27, no. 2, Summer 2015, pp. 285-304.

Rifenburgh, Dan. "What Is Poetry?" *National Endowment for the Arts.* Operation Homecoming, NEA, 2012, https://www.arts.gov/operation-homecoming/essays-writing/what-poetry. Accessed 5 Aug. 2018.

Rodríguez, R. Joseph. "Our US Poet Laureate and Hispanic Heritage." *Literacy and NCTE: The Official Blog of the National Council of Teachers of English*, 22 Sept. 2015. http://www2.ncte.org/blog/2015/09/hispanic-heritage/. Accessed 7 Aug. 2018.

Rodríguez, R. Joseph. "Variation on a Theme by Lucille Clifton." Unpublished poem.

Rosaldo, Renato. *The Day of Shelly's Death: The Poetry and Ethnography of Grief.* Duke UP, 2014.

Sáenz, Benjamin Alire. *The Book of What Remains.* Copper Canyon P, 2010.

—. *Dark and Perfect Angels: A Collection of Poems.* Cinco Puntos P, 1995.

Saint-Exupéry, Antoine de. *The Little Prince.* 1943. Translated by Richard Howard. Houghton Mifflin Harcourt, 2000.

Scenters-Zapico, Natalie. *The Verging Cities: Poems.* UP of Colorado and Utah State UP, 2015.

Staudt, Kathleen, and Zulma Y. Méndez. *Courage, Resistance, and Women in Ciudad Juárez: Challenges to Militarization.* U of Texas

P, 2015.

Permissions

Andrea Blancas Beltran, "Reading and Writing Lessons" from *Acentos Review*, Feb. 2013. The poem is reprinted by permission from Andrea Blancas Beltran.

Jorge A. Gómez, "Mexadus" from *Acentos Review*, May 2013. The poem is reprinted by permission from Jorge A. Gómez.

Rafael Jesús González, "Las Torres" from *Abalone Moon: A Journal of Poetry and the Arts*, Fall 2007, November 6, 2007. The poem is reprinted by permission from Rafael Jesús González.

Rafael Jesús González, "The Towers" from *Abalone Moon: A Journal of Poetry and the Arts*, Fall 2007, November 6, 2007. The poem is reprinted by permission from Rafael Jesús González.

Sheryl Luna, "Lowering Your Standards for Food Stamps." Copyright © 2014, by Sheryl Luna. Originally published in *Poetry*, April 2014. The poem is reprinted by permission of Sheryl Luna.

Pat Mora, "Bribe" from *Chants* and *My Own True Name: New and Selected Poems for Young Adults, 1984–1999*. Copyright © 1984, 1994, 2000, by Pat Mora. The poem is reprinted by permission from Pat Mora and Arte Público Press, Piñata Books, Houston, Texas.

R. Joseph Rodríguez, "at Sierra de los Mansos" from "Our US Poet Laureate and Hispanic Heritage," *Literacy and NCTE: The Official Blog of the National Council of Teachers of English,* September 22, 2015. The poem is reprinted by permission from R. Joseph Rodríguez and the National Council of Teachers of English (NCTE), Urbana, Illinois.

POETRY

JONATHAN BRACKER

Cheerful, and Its Alternative

Cheerful is near.
It is not far away like happiness.
It is something we make for ourselves

Because we can. Dour, cheerful's alternative,

Works also—and tempts, requiring no thought
Or effort. Sometimes almost a lifetime must be lived
Before we may discover the better one to choose.

Two Views of Away

I am eight or nine and we are in the kitchen
Shelling peas. Mother hands me the heavy sky-blue bowl
Of jade-green snaps, explaining in detail how to do it.
Grammaw, Mother's mother, died last week.
Doing for the first time this task, I am able to ask
"Death—what does it mean?" I very much want to know.

Mother has been watching to see whether I open my pods correctly.
"Death," she almost immediately replies,
Having no need to stop and think, "is just like
Someone being away on a trip."
Surprised, I do not believe this
For a moment.

Now I am older than she was then. A rich friend having once more
Been flown over the Atlantic Ocean to new lands,
Being someone who likes to keep on the move as long as he can,
I the left-behind buddy feel how when a dear one is away
It is a kind of death till he comes back. Friends do come back,
But I very much dislike this feeling—always have, and always will!

Into Later Life

What do people take with them into later life?

Elderly Annie has taken a plastic napkin ring
In the shape of an elephant
Glossy and hard to the touch
With a large hole in the middle of its flatness
For a neatly rolled-up cloth to stick out equally on either side,
Given her at six by dear tall goofy Aunt Marie.

What Annie likes about the elephant with minimal tail
And only slightly indicated ears
Is its butterscotch color and the fact that its eyes
Are a ruby red insert
That you may push in and out with finger and thumb,
Which she still finds pleasant to do.

For awhile today Annie cannot recall its location.
Where has she displayed the ring for others to see?
(She scatters toys and little dolls about the apartment
For visitors to pick up and observe if they wish.)
Butterscotch elephants do not just disappear.
Surely she has not thrown it away,
Or given it to somebody else?

Gladly now Annie spies her pachyderm
Upright atop the bookcase in the hall
Where she had placed it near the hook for apartment keys
So that, going into the neighborhood,
Out of the corner of her seventy-nine-year-old eye
She can relish its stolid vivacity. She is relieved,
Because mostly it is there for her to see.

When It Is Time to Get Up

Perhaps when you were quite young
And so much smaller than you are now
Your mother made you nap in the afternoon.
You were restless, and wanted to get up
From the mattress on the sun porch floor:
Socks and shoes off, wearing just your little skirt
Or short pants, with a soft cotton shirt on your chest,
Your legs tricycling, your heels drumming
Against enforced inactivity, you called
"Is it time for me to get up yet?" and she called back
"Stay where you are, I'll tell you when it is."

That did happen to me.

But today, as on other wakings at this point in my old life
I was tempted to stay in bed longer than eight hours, wishing
To burrow under the bedclothes like some instinctive furry creature
Eager to stay warm in winter. Yet I knew better. I got up
And after awhile, when I had done what I have learned to do
(Put bedclothes away, pull curtains open, go to the bathroom
To wash my face and clean my teeth and use a nailbrush on my fingers
As Mother and Daddy and my sister had done) found
What I had hoped to find: old-fashioned cheerfulness;
And I wanted to tell you
How I have learned to awake.

That Old Gang of Mine

Its arms nearly grazing the city building
Which I apartment in, a mature tree
(Perhaps wild plum
Though the fruit it bears
Is shaped like a kind of
Cherry) gives solid pleasure.

In February the fruit
Glistens for only a week,
Then falls
To get trounced. But the leaves,
A similar kind of reddish purple,
Remain.

For one day only, in the spring of two different years,
I have watched within it the jostling existence
Of active and communicative
Small yellow birds.
Now that I am eighty-one
I want to see just such a gang of migrant

Non-laborers (neither toilers
Nor spinners), round little yellow
Bundles, hop again. I resolve to remember
To next February keep my eyes peeled
For a possible dropping-by
Once more of that community.

MICHAEL CERAOLO

Five from _Eighty Days_

July 19, 1881

Garfield:

What with my wounds
being described in graphic detail,
and the talk of my constant cheerfulness,
"I should think the public would be tired
of having me dished up to them in this way"

Guiteau:

"I thought the Deity and I had done it"

July 20, 1881

Garfield:

"There are times
in the history of men and nations,
when they stand so near the veil
that separates mortals and immortals,
time from eternity,
and men from their God,
that they can almost hear their breathings
and feel the pulsations
of the heart of the infinite"

I leave it to others to decide
if this is one of those times for our nation,
but it is one of those times for me

Guiteau:

"The idea
that I was to be eternally damned
haunted me
and haunted me
and haunted me
every day" for many years,
but I overcame it and was able
to go about my business

July 21, 1881

Garfield:

Today I discharged
a large quantity of pus from the wound
(I occasionally find myself
lapsing into medical jargon)
Interesting to me
was the fact that in the drained pus
was a one-inch square of my clothing,
a piece pushed into my body by the bullet,,
the bullet still remaining inside me

Guiteau:

"I shot the President as I would a rebel,
if I saw him pulling down the American flag
I leave my justification
to God and the American people"

July 22, 1881

Garfield:

I asked one of those attending me
"What was probably
the central velocity of the bullet?"
I got no answer,
but
if an answer is ever found
I should like to know it

Guiteau:

The gun I used was a
.44-caliber British Bulldog revolver,
self-cocking,
with an ivory handle that will look good
when the gun is exhibited in a museum

July 23, 1881

Garfield:

"I am too tired
to portray the workings of my mind,
which have been numerous"

I will resume tomorrow

Guiteau:

"I had something in me
and had to get it out...
went lecturing,
but I had little reputation
and I had but little success

People did not want to hear me"

LOUIS GALLO

Wittgenstein: A Micro-Biography

The young man detested their silly giggling in the cafes.
Bright ribbons fluttered in the usual girls' hair.
Psychoanalysts passed in silken, black carriages.
Assassination and hemophilia troubled the empire.
A new theory of light drove him into cold, dim rooms.
He stood on a corner in Vienna and felt inches shorter.
A horse snorted. The new century severed time like an ax.
"Reality begets language!" he cried to no one.

That same reality betrayed him. He never smiled,
stroked a severe violin as his brothers killed themselves.
His youthful decorum hardened into zeal
and he listened for breathing beneath the ink.
He imagined words so refined they split throats
even as safer, more prudent words floated
through his mind like balloons. He was wrong.
There was only language.
He stopped talking and disappeared for years.

Then we find him sulking on the patios of wry philologists.
The infinite but unbounded universe had expanded.
War hero, school master, common gardener,
he entertained the philological wives:
"Philosophy," he teased, "is a battle against
the bewitchment of an intelligence by means of language."
He accompanied students to Walt Disney movies
in a personal dome of gloom, insisting his aim
was "to show the fly the way out of the fly bottle."
On the day he died he shot up in bed, wild-eyed,
beseeched his last disciple, "Tell them I've lived
a wonderful life!"

The Charm of Fine Manners

I bought a book today from a quaint bookshop
tucked away in the mountains, a store with
little traffic, tended by a meticulous bookseller.
The book, *The Charm of Fine Manners*
by Helen Eking Starrett, Director of the
Starrett School for Girls, had been preserved
with what we used to call "loving care."
I bought it because I wanted to improve
my etiquette in my dotage. It had lagged
behind for decades.
Of course, the book was published in 1907
and thereby woefully outdated—precisely
why I wanted it: that old-fashioned sense
of decorum and propriety, however absurd.
According to the author our chief virtues
are order, neatness, promptness and cheerfulness.
As I read, I observed the chaotic disarray
of my study; as for neatness, I believe it
intimately linked to order. Promptness?
It's 2018! I'm reading it over a hundred years
later. Cheerfulness—who has world enough
and time? Or cause? Cheer: *go Tigers go*!
Let's consult Schopenhauer and Wittgenstein.
I slide the book onto my shelf between
"Journey to the End of Night" and "Flowers
of Evil." It looks good there, cheerful.

Thales

this the Ionian who claimed
that everything was made of water
(Heraclitus vouched for fire)

but if water we must take into account
condensation, evaporation & carbonation
all three of which have always
intrigued me

don't you know people who condense,
who smear themselves all over
a surface
or those who merely evaporate?

carbonation—a slightly different deal
since it involves gas
(and there was another Ionian
who made that claim for everything)

but those who carbonate
rather than evaporate
man they go out in style
all those sizzling bubbles
and hiss
what razzmatazz!
what crazy style!

but really
I like the fiery angle too—
and they say Heraclitus
was a most disagreeable man

Scherzo Furiant—America Now

I listen to the glorious fourth movement
of the Sixth Symphony and wonder
what the hell Anton Dvorak was doing
in Spillsville, Iowa, in 1893.
Kolaces, polkas, pilsener...
he loved the place and listened
as the Dubuque Symphony performed
The New World in a high school gym.
He fished in the Turkey River
and instructed Americans that
they had better heed black and
native American music:
there was the soul of the USA.
In the end he missed Bohemia
and returned home to the ancient,
surreal, tragic, passionate origin
of Czechoslovakia.
Sometimes I wonder what I too
am doing in America, especially now.
I have no Czech accouterments
except a few pair of old glass
Mardi Gras beads crafted in that country
decades ago. Or make it some stone,
solemn church in Armenia where
women in black shawls rub their rosaries
in avid precision. No scherzo furiant—
only centuries of mute grief.
Grave New World.

Linguistics

Signifier beat his breast in triumph,
cartwheeled around the stadium
and saluted himself in a distorting mirror.
Only I, he proclaimed. How he disdained
what he arbitrarily signified, how that
bastardized unknown taunted him
with its claim to essence.

Signified pities Signifier and laughs.
Mere babble, that other, random gutturals
and sibilants with no claim.
I am the claim. Dress me as you will.
Nobody knows me—I, the *ding an sich,*
ha ha, your hell and your heaven.
Look, what you call a bluebird
perches upon what you call a branch
of what you call a weeping willow.
Translation, bah, you will never see,
grasp, touch, taste or touch the rara avis.

Latin

Caesar, of course, with Gaul
and its three partes,
and Horace, the *dulce et decorum est*
(see also Wilfred Owen)
though I hated the *pro patria mori*
business—
Mr. Casanova, no joke, Tulane
at something Hall on the Newcomb
campus, he a real Italian with heavy
dark-blue proto-whiskers
but no beard (though no razor
could bleach the blue-black.
Oh he hated teaching declensions
and conjugations and I hated
trying to understand—
a nice, sweet man, however macho
he looked, joshing with us students
as we agonized over Vergil
(that second-rate Homer
with his dildo, I mean, Dido)
and SextusPropertius
...but I knew enough to translate
some Milton for my MA degree
or rather the professor passed me
because I really didn't know enough.
Sad, because I love Latin, learned
more about English from it
than Latin itself. *Hic et nunc,*
in medias res, in illo tempore—
man, the easy ones.
Latin, like sex in the
passive pluperfect subjunctive...
(not *amo, amas, amat*)

with the coldest woman
you've ever known.

Sprocket

I like the clickety verve of the word "sprocket."
It's how you savor words. Forget the signifieds,
go for the hum, music and jangle, the meat.
Forget what you're eating; regard the packaging
though at some point you must rip it and mind
the mimicry. I don't like the words "turbine," "rubric"
(except when it suggests Rubicon), "margarine,"
nor the name "Nancy." Who knows why?
As a kid I hated peanut butter but things change.
My students prefer French—*casa*, house, *maison*—
they always choose *maison*. And *deliquescence*,
avilissement (for which no swanky equivalent
exits in Anglo-Saxon). "Weltanschuauung"—
God have mercy. German doesn't move me,
"heil," though "tod" as in Venice has its
grotesque charm. The Slavic *litost* has merit—
but pray you don't get litosted.
I'm reading about extinct languages—
Sumerian, proto-Indo-European, Etruscan
and so many more. Here's a tomb inscription
from Etruscan translated into English:
"avils LX lupuce"—he lived 60 years.
All those lost words can make one weep.
Think of the missing poetry, the urgent messages
never delivered, a pining lover leaping
into Etna because he never received the valentine.
Maybe each of us who has ever lived
amounts to one word (I hope I'm not "turbine")
in our vast missive to God, a verbal sprocket
that perhaps God never reads because He or She
is illiterate or blind. And here we are, yapping
away for millennia, the old sound and fury.
I really like the word "fetor" and its adjective—

"fetid." Say it aloud... so perfect, so apt.
And here's where signifier slides into signified,
yin/yang, the eternal OM, white light
that contains all colors, even the Shadow.

Hauntology: Origin

I wish Derrida wrote more beautifully
because this idea, while wrong, is beautiful—
no tracing an origin without seeking
a further origin. Sounds like Godel's Theorem
of systems always leaking into higher systems
or Aquinas panting after God in that endless
successions of greater Goods. Russian
stack boxes full of cupcakes.
Or maybe it's not wrong after all. Maybe
the origin is *hic et nunc*—(on which see
Gebser's *Ever Present Origin*.) Alpha
and omega fused in the present moment
which, once stated as present, is past.
I like it. We all contain the Big Bang,
which is the Ur origin, right? unless
we ask what came before the Bang—
apparently nothing, a void, phantom
fluctuations of virtual particles, one
of which corporealized. Which? Why?
Well, I'm haunted. *Haunto, Hauntas,*
Hauntat, Hauntamus, Hauntatis, Hauntant.
Freud said, "He who inquires into the meaning
of life is sick." Count me sick. I crave knowing
what it's all about, Algae, I mean Alfie.
Otherwise we're hula hooping in quicksand
on borrowed time without life jackets.
Could be worse, could be the birds
in my back yard pecking at a seed bell,
not one tiny husk of an idea. Worse, eh?

Fyodor

While consummating the marriage
with his new, young wife
Dostoevsky endured an epileptic fit,
foamed at the mouth, was flung
off the bed to lie unconscious
on the floor, stiff as concrete.
I like to think that in such a state
he remembered the wall,
the seven muskets aimed at his heart
for his dabbling with socialism.
At the last minute his sentence
was commuted and he wound up
cursed with hard labor in some place
like Siberia. Imagine, Dostoevsky
condemned to hard labor!
Yet he survived and as the epilepsy
progressed he became renowned
for ferocious even violent sexual prowess.
His mistresses claimed that it was as if
he coaxed the seizures on to assure them
the most passionate, memorable sex
they could possibly imagine—as if
they were conjoined with a volcano.
I don't know if all of this is true,
but some of it is…
and parts always signify wholes.
All the while Father Zosima's corpse
still stinks up the chapel.

Ergo Sum

That's the part that haunts me, has
haunted me for decades, the ergo sum,
as it implies that what doesn't think—
say, plants, rocks, water, earth itself—
doesn't exist, and yet we know they exist,
don't we? Dr. Johnson kicking the rock,
for instance—Berkeley refuted, instantly,
and yet... if we attribute varied degrees
of consciousness even to plants and rock
and Omnia as would the shamans and animists
(those myriad river gods, the Roman lemurs)
we might get away with it except that quantum
physics wants to shindig now with the philosophers:
the Copenhagen School, the most Prussian
and conservative (and I stress conservative)
with its impeccable equations stipulating that
(1) either an infinity of worlds co-exists
with the one we think we're in or (2) we, US,
"create" reality by merely observing it, the
participatory business, the latter verified
by something called "the collapse of the wave
function," from Schrodinger, whose cat
figures into all this by being dead and alive
at once and either meets the "true death"
(ah, I miss "True Blood") or the true life
when someone opens the lid. Observes.
So what to make of all this, let's face it,
preposterous speculation? Descartes,
no fool, saw angels. So did Newton, that
sublime yet paranoid mind. Dr. Johnson,
well, just a good old boy at heart—didn't
realize or care that the rock was mostly
empty space however much it stubbed his toe.

And Schrodinger, how dream up the "collapse"
and then prove it mathematically?
Was that poetry or hallucination or revelation?
Could any of us have thought that one up?
Kant's thing in itself turns out to be NO-thing
but an infinite (?) field of energy, radiation,
potential… and thus we somehow emerge
from it to become US and thereby we observe
part of the energy left behind and, voila,
the world—lamp posts, magnolia trees, the
Tower of Pisa (Pizza?), the shrimp po-boy
I crave. But we've drifted… Rene, back to you:
you forever divided the mind and the body
(though many now say you were utterly wrong),
so, for me, you have made such bestowal
and do I like it or not? Who knows? MWF
I like it… but does it imply that when we're not
thinking, say, when asleep or zonked in comas,
we don't exist? That's what you're saying, man,
and it sounds more crazy than me here
trying to figure it out, thinking about it,
Cogito, my ass (who observed it to create it?)

Archetypes

We bandy about the term as if
we know what we're talking about.
We don't. Nobody does.
Freud said the unconscious mind
is structured like jokes; Jung said
like alchemic transformations.
I say it's structured like chaos, what
the early Americans called "howling wilderness."
Probe that dream you had of driving
along a steep cliff during a mudslide.

Are they endemic to the mind or
to the universe? Did the Ice Man
harken to the moon as I did the other night?
I like to think both, but it makes no difference
since we sift the universe through
our very neurons and can't probe it
any other way—that outer extremity.

Jung says one thing, Eliade another
though I like Jung: "there is good reason
for supposing that the archetypes are the
 unconscious images of the instincts themselves,
 in other words, that they are patterns
of instinctual behaviour." Good—that means
I myself, and you too, are (y)our own archetypes.
Oh Susana! How I fear the Shadow
but adore the Wise Old Man and the Babe.

Did Bach pluck that motet I listened to
repeatedly as a child out of the cosmos
or did the cosmos feed it into his gray brain
so he could bestow it upon all of us?
The man accosted women in the chapel
on the pipe organ itself. Should we think
less of him for that? I guess so, but that motet
is so beautiful I cringe to hear it. Sacred,
it's sacred.

Excise that banjo out of my heart
so I can plunk out another Doo—Dah.
There's an archetype for you.

SUSIE GHARIB

Beyond Repair

My friends are sewing away
at tattered matrimony
fiddling with pieces that are through wear
torn
threadbare
beyond repair
the children nestling to their au pair
gasping for air
with the fixed stare.

Tinkering away at splintered rhetoric
historic
supersonic,
the gods meddle with a state of affairs
beyond repair
their surrealistic version of elegant warfare
growing pale.

Toying with disjointed verse
a poet hankers after rhyme
in modern times
bandaging so many disfigured lines
craving for a metrical alliance
the resurrection after a long demise.

Plaintive

My new employment is in an antique shop
it was my interest in the historic novel
that helped me obtain the job
he asked which novel appealed to me most
Ivanhoe was my shot
Richard the Lionhearted and Templar Knights
animate its world
he commended my taste
and asked me to instantly commence my work
which consists of offering assistance to his wealthy fops.

An architect of some renown
takes to my total indifference to men
and invites me to Loch Lomond over the weekend.

The serenity with which his eyes dwell
on the inhabitants of the lake
is that of a Celtic sage
a Druidic gaze.

We sit on a protruding rock
as ancient as age
and though his use of words is sparse
he has a presence
that keeps every fiber in my system
aesthetically awake
warmth begins seeping into my veins.

The screams of restless seagulls rend the air.

'Plaintive,' say I, amazed.
'Plaintive is the word,' answers he,
with eyes dwelling on my enraptured face.

A single word would suffice for the day.

The pebbled shores of Loch Lomond
and a seat of rock
have ever since become my Camelot.

A Dormant Door Mat

Her slumber remains unruffled by paws and feet
her face, grown ashen, prematurely aged
with hair so bristly like a stubbly beard,
dreaming of smudges from rain-drenched streets
of thrills from spanks with sticks, and flips
of the garden hose cleansing her clogged pores
of the inevitable sun-bathing on a low-statured wall
of the graffiti on the ancient front gate:
'HAUNTED, and Please Not for Sale'
and she knows that ghosts leave no foot-prints
not even in dreams.

A Lateen Sail

Moored to the left
on a turquoise dress
a lateen sail
was the birthday gift
Lucia could not have anticipated.

It was not the gold
with which it was forged
that enthralled the heart
of a three-year-old
rather the triangle
and the sea evoked.

Attuned to the rhythmic
ebbs and flows
of an ocean of breaths
heaving below
it dropped its anchor
on the floor
where paper-boats
had found repose
nestling to weed
to kelp
to pearls
curling within
neat graves
of grass.

The sail was sold
with things of worth
when Lucia could not
have argued its cause
losing the broche
when a five-year-old.

Fifty years had passed
but the anchor holds fast
to the ocean-bed
of a steadfast heart
a coral shrine
to the bearer of gift,
Paulette.

ROB LUKE

The Reckoning of Rabbit

In Beverly Farms, Massachusetts
searching for John Updike's ghost.
His name etched on the public library.
The librarian pledging that the author
had been private yet polite. He, the
clairvoyant of Harry "Rabbit"
Angstrom, the everyman zombie,
controlled by the voodoo of former
high school basketball stardom
and interludes of hollowing
sexual gratification—neither
lasting adulation.

Oh, Rabbit, John Updike breathing
booze scented breath into your
character. After adolescent
notoriety dissipated, you followed
your father into the profession of
linotype, setting metal letters gave
you the skill to read sideways and
upside down, skewing your perspective.
Working hard, you eked out a living
until muscled out by my generation's
vocational offset printing. My eyes
dimmed lithographic stripping film over a
light table, wearing my pupils out, though
reading literature would have been a far
nobler sacrifice of vision.

Oh, Rabbit, your birth and rank
saved when your father-in-law tossed
you a fraying rope of financial stability.
Your clay flesh, ever yearning to return
to the garden of a gnarly tree,
transformed into assembly line
Japanese plastic, as you hawked Toyotas.
Empty jock itch replaced by sexual
showroom conquests.

Oh, Rabbit, the only parallel to my
own father was your passivity that could
blaze into violence. Oh, Rabbit, both of
you did what you perceived as right.
Later, in your dying days, looking for
elusive sunlight to make sense of your
lives. Returning to the scenes of
stuck throttles: a basketball court for
Rabbit and cancer ward morphine
recollections for my dad.
My dad mouthing the words of the
Lord's Prayer as his pastor's
voice rang out with clarity.
"Forgive us our trespasses as
we forgive those who trespass
against us." Oh, Rabbit, not your
problem.

Oh, Rabbit, even my English methods
professor, who chucked Christianity,
hated you for running, Oh, Rabbit,
you claimed to believe in God
and country, though both more
fizz than substance in your libations.
Oh, Rabbit, you are not an everyman:
you are a nobody.

TOM MCFADDEN

Sharing Rain

It began as dream quest.
Flowing downward inside the crowd on the turning stairs
as classes left out in the old college building,
my eyes fell upon her, ahead of me,
and in that special moment on the tenuous stairs
I dreamed I could feel tomorrow.
Outside, although through a sudden fear of the unrequited,
I managed to create engagement,
and, happily, became allowed to walk her home, to her apartment,
down what turned out to be our shared street.
When we stopped before her door,
I forced myself once more through fear,
proposing the chance of our first sharing.
Yet, when "the love of my life" said "no,"
alone I soon stood in the early winter chill
while the lonely sidewalk stretched away,
into its symbolic emptiness.
Later, I walked back from my own apartment
to stare at her second-floor window,
with the darkness it framed for me
as my portrait of the unrequited,
once more to walk away, into the sidewalk's emptiness.
Yet, what had always saved me
was the wonderful world of the arts.
I knew I was a wordsmith,
and over the weeks I composed my heart in words
to give her, who chose to read it.
Now time has journeyed these fifty years.
Through the glass, slide door of the back yard
and through the fall of light raindrops,

illogically there she is,
her hand happily casting bird seed
into spots in the grass.
Surprised, and returned from another room,
I see that the innocent face
beneath the long-brimmed, straw hat
does not seem to know it is lightly raining.
With a lucid glance at the drops,
off course I know,
but I must know it alone,
for the love of my life is on early miles
of her journey into Alzheimer's,
beyond the exactness of the day.
Yet, through the illogic
and through the inclemency,
I see only my miracle,
for we live, still, in the house as two,
and there can I see her through the glass, slide door.
So, I pull a cap from the hallway closet,
then go outside, too.
Through the grass and birdseed I walk to her side.
Then, although with perspectives not quite the same,
together we share the unknown rain.

Note-Ride

The door of the jazz club opened
into an ambience of aesthetic feel,
as though an avenue of chance,
then availed a sense of slow passage through translucence
among the tight tables
while a bass guitar, drums, and a piano in the far corner
articulated sonic reach toward the ineffable.
Varied faces rode the note-ride,
some swept into could-come-true
while others, more pained, fell into
a reflective wondering of what might have transpired
during their own reach for life's music.
Over the mist of countenances traveled the notes,
as though the instruments had voices,
while faces listened, then empathized
with the sweep of exploration,
as if the air of the setting
did traverse an aesthetic avenue.
Over future-cast wishes
and over invisible scars
floated the sonic review
while a little boy, as sent participant,
walked happily to piano's end
to drop a five into the glass jar of thanks,
then returned to his table, smiling.
High notes and low notes seemed journey
through life's imperfection,
weaving among the biographies,
until, abruptly, as the door opened for others to enter,
notes touched dreams and remembrances once more,
then drifted through the doorway
into the rhythm of the night.

The Night Is a Poem

We have settled into quiet wait
on our backyard, fold-up chairs
to sit inside the fall of hours—
to read the biography of the sky
and vicariously join the fall of light.
While blue above lingers undisturbed,
the moment begins to disappoint
as a literature uninformed of passion.
Yet, abruptly, instincts alert us to reread the sky,
and we slowly discern the blue realm's yield
to orange-red beauty above us
in an awe-inspiring evolution of colors and tints.
Beneath the canopy,
the microcosm of our own emotions
feels led by the sky,
and we seem to fall under its spell.
Dreams feel allowed once more to live in reality
with happiness welcomed
until...
the orange-red canopy begins to lessen in its existence,
ultimately fading into a debility of pink,
then into an unwelcome sharing with streaks of gray,
and finally into only ominous gray.
Our tilted-high countenances turn commensurate
with subtle impulses of foreboding,
and, while we stare at the sky,
we wonder if we read our dreams' dissuasion.
Yet, full blackness develops above us,
then looms in place not in foretelling,
but only as mystery, vast and magnificent.
We stare at it, unable to read a literature so grand.
The sight is wondrous in its strength—
deep in its wealth of enigmatic quality

and its offer only of wondering.
And, suddenly, as I stare at and feel it
while it touches my face,
I realize that
the night is a poem.

ANDREW ALEXANDER MOBBS

What Happens When the Sun Dies

"Scientists agree the sun will die in approximately five billion years, but they weren't sure what would happen next—until now."
    —University of Manchester (from "What will happen when our sun dies?" on Science Daily)

I. *Envelope Ejection*

After eons of radiating heat to warm our
brittle bodies, inspiring artists and heliologists

in their creations and research, serving as a
deity for everyone from ancient Egyptians to

Greeks to Native American tribes, curbing
our depressive tendencies with vitamin D-rich

rays, and illuminating the skies just because
it can, there comes a time in the sun's life

when it must part ways with its mass of gas and
dust, ship its chemical compositions on paper boats

into the colorless abyss. Only then will its true
core be revealed and begin to degenerate over

the course of 10,000 years—a mere blink in the
astronomical eye—naked, exposed, free.

II. *Nebular Aftermath*

When the envelope shines, the solar ghost
is born. Whoever is alive will see it from tens of

millions of light years away, outshining even
its own former body. Envision Apollo clearing out

his things for Hades, trading the safe predictability
of golden warmth for the captivating emptiness

contained within the nearly incomprehensible
circumference of a luminous ring of interstellar

matter the color of our tears. A planetary nebula
is what scientists say, but what they really mean

is a postpartum sun, lamenting the photons it kept
like children, coping with a slow, marvelous death.

III. *Farewell, Earth*

See the paradox: our terra-bound days are
numbered, yet numbers are infinite. See the

paradox: all things made of matter will no longer
matter. See the paradox: before the next lifeform

can thrive, the current lifeform must perish. If we
cannot keep the earth, we cannot keep our earthly

memories. Billions of area codes and historical
dates will evaporate. All the first steps, kisses, and

junior high heartbreaks will be lost in a black hole
of consciousness. Words like *inconsequential*

will become inconsequential. Even as I finish this
poem, I watch the hungry flames dance around it.

Habitable Worlds That Have No Sun

"It is thought that, throughout the universe, there are former moons that were once part of planetary systems but now wander, rogue and alone."
—*Chelsea Gohd (from "The Universe May Be Full of Habitable Worlds That Have No Sun")*

I once lived on a starless ex-moon
beneath a mesh-pocked sky

that let everything from dark matter
to photons from god

knows where seep into the atmosphere,
diffuse through my being, and

I couldn't fathom how warm it was
without a sun, how there could

possibly be water to slake my thirst,
and I never questioned why

my *luna non grata* of a world
was shunned so biblically from the

once-loving embrace of its planetary
family, whether it was paying

the price for some cosmic fuckup
or was simply Judas-kissed

by gravity, but even now, other bodies
are floating out there, outcasts

tethered in the same pristine blackness,
trading tidal friction for heat,

inching closer together, slower
than timid lovers in the dark

craving that nearness, that feeling
of each other's breath

against their own innocent skin,
waiting to rebel against the star-orbiting

systems the best way they know how:
existing,
alone.

Lessons from an Orca: Tonic Immobility

Everything begins with a hunger so visceral, a hunger that engulfs its nine-meter, nine-ton body like the current itself, a hunger that foreshadows poetic justice where predator becomes prey. Any size advantage is incidental. Sleek and salt-tinged in the afternoon sun, the orca propels itself at a striking speed through the water with its fins splayed in utter surrender. Perpendicularly, it rams the side of the unsuspecting shark, Titanic-like, flipping it over to where its vast white stomach kisses the surface one final time. The orca is nothing if not patient; it will hold the shark in place for up to half an hour, relishing its catatonia, whispering to the increasingly cold-blooded creature with its obsidian eyes, *No movement, no breath, this is how you greet your death.* When the time is right, the orca slices through the cartilage like sword against silk, devouring the nutrient-rich liver, slaking its bloodthirst, watching as the carcass sinks to the black depths from which it came.

Lessons from a Bottlenose Dolphin: Echolocation

Odontocetes are no different from humans; we both speculate pains-takingly about the unknown. Despite its vocal cordless larynx, the bot-tlenose dolphin is born with two distinct phonologic lips that channel air through its nasal passage to produce sound in such a way that it can whistle and click simultaneously at frequencies shooting through the water nearly five times faster than air. An aural birthmark, each dol-phin's whistle is so unique that the creature itself can be identified via sonogram. Sometimes, when the dolphin is cutting through the dark depths of the sea, it echolocates to determine whether or not it's alone and unthreatened. This goes both ways; the hungrier the dolphin, the easier it is for their brains to recognize signals reflected off the skulls of their unsuspecting prey, mesmerized by the loud impulse sounds, paus-ing for a crucial moment just long enough to wonder what could have been as the dolphin's rostrum opens like a drawbridge.

What Crosses the Mind of a Bird in a Storm

"Even the hard winter... has been followed by an eruption of song from our feathered friends."
-L. Michael Romero, Professor of Biology

If I survive to see just one more spring, sharing
these microhabitats will have been worthwhile.

*

To those who hunker with me, hearts beating
fast in manzanita thickets, notches of spruce:

*

there's no shame in conceding our species is
vulnerable, that our bones can snap like tooth-

*

picks in the perfect recipe of raging winds. Since
when was anything more than blood flow & a

*

few tendons strung together? I accept this storm
as my savior in whose name I adapt, trapping

*

air in my feathers, creating a masterpiece of
equilibrium within my five-ounce body, amen.

                        *

When the air pressure changes slightly or my
hatchlings chirp from their pine-needled nest,

                    *

I give in to the yearning that pulsates through
my microscopic veins, becoming exactly what

                *

I was designed to be: a fierce flash of indigo
cutting the troposphere, dark-eyed, laughing

            *

madly as it struggles to sew itself up, fumbling
the sutures with clumsy, rain-slickened hands.

TIMOTHY ROBBINS

Happy at Last

Before you chanced on me on the friary
stoop (Oh! It sounds like I'm a foundling
and you're the Little Tramp!) it was

enough to collect pairs of similarities,
never before paired. Before you
confiscated my cap and put it on

your head, lifted the guitar from my lap and
put it to bed, it was enough to breed new
colors and name them after temps I hired

and fired for their more than bread alone.
We tiptoed up the stairs and
down the hall with the tacit approval of

a handful of monks whose sleeping
sensuality stirred and made infant-like
sounds. Approval? Nay, applause for it

was no longer enough to lead raindrops
in their prayers, to seek out recent widows
and take their mourning unawares, to

know the world through naked palms and
naked soles. As I will never get
enough of you, nothing is whole.

Fußball

The rod through the foosballers'
hips kept them together safely apart.
This inspired your movement for prison
reform. What if I walked around
licking every cheek in the room?
What if I told the Born Agains their
Holy Lord was dead again? What if
you found out those hard little plastic
athletes were cheating?
You make the mistake of thinking all
dreamers are optimists. Discipline the
banjo. It will discipline you in return.
Tune the power lines gradually or
they'll snap and stab your eye. The sky
tilts. Clouds slide like deck furniture
on a listing ship. Unlike angels, demons,
gods, these folding chairs can't scramble
for higher decks or fight for a lifeboat.
There stands your destiny, doubting
your reality. Go to it. Lift the hair
from its neck. Kiss the soft and the hard
behind its ear.

The Informer

I'm thinking of something
more domestic. I become

my best quiet. I sit on the
carpet at a low table. The

town is waking in front
of me. Mike is preparing

coffee behind my back.
The microwave closes

with a commanding clack.

Inside Outside

In the picture you're in
a box. The box
represents a cage.
(The offspring of
hyper-realistic paintings,
 I love and hate
representational art.)
I admit I
drew the box. I
even admit to
some vanity at
how well it's drawn.
Though really
how hard is it to
draw a box well? Where
the cage came from
and how you wound
up inside it,
I've been trying to
tell for twenty years.
How many times
have I pointed out:
removing you
disposing of the box
would be easy?
"Stupid artist," you say,
"That's irrelevant
and irreverent
to the cage that is me."

Judy

The first night in Byron's dorm room our
amazed exuberance was audible to the
boy with whom he shared a phone box.
Maybe his neighbor's reaction (Lysol on
the swivel phone) was purely hygienic.

Maybe Lysol was the closest cleanser he
had to mace. It was 1983 and facing this
guy in the shower was a feat of everyday
activism my harpsichordist didn't care
o embrace. While we strategized, an

irate mob of crickets stridulated outside
the low (as though made to facilitate
cricket invasions) windows. We thought it
best to make like germs and let the spray
efface us. This is how his bosom pal

Judy came to lend us her bedroom for
a month. She slept on the sofa, got up
early to make breakfast for three with a
glee I never understood. We laughed at the
irony every time we screwed as quietly as

we could and thought we should. "The
walls have ears—fag hag ears," you
whispered. Actually the walls were brick.
Bricks I wanted to live behind when I
walked past the Gilliland's ivy-besieged

house on the way to kid's hour at the
library. Bricks the Hebrews baked for the
Pharaoh. Bricks that reminded me of
soldiers' names on all four sides of my
hometown square. In my imagination,

AIDS victim bricks, Holocaust victim
bricks. How long would Judy Feinstein
have let Byron Schenkman and his Goy-
friend stay? Too long. Ten Plagues
would not have made her kick us out.

ROBERT RONNOW

Rhodora in Winter

Rhodora in winter, capsule like a claw,
remains of the 5-part flower Emerson saw,
gone to seed. Deciduous trees and shrubs
have their own winter beauty and a power
akin to the fittest's survival, self-same
that brought me, musing, here. Large globose buds!
(that dwarf the rose's but not the butternut's)
distinguish it from other Ericaceae that
surround this inland wetland. The Lord
all claim to worship is not better
than thou. I'm passing through naming you,
your parts, and the autumn elaeagnus who
is your neighbor. Good a walk as it gets
before edible understory herbs sprout.

Peace Out

I can't blame the teenage girl for being forward,
then passive aggressive. It shouldn't make one angry;
she has her interests and that which bores her.

Or the adolescent boy for being antsy, a little loopy
and aloof. Under that hat he wants to be good,
is deeply disappointed with the world (and the food).

Robert Francis: the finest poet no one reads.
We care not. Such prisms of philosophy need
no acknowledgment. The catamount is only believed

to be extinct. The wildlife tree, a mere bole,
deep in the forest, far off the road, when it falls
takes many squirrel turbines and spider spans down with it.

Noon, Julian has nothing much to do
and likes it that way. That way nothing much gets done today.
Every man, every tree, lives with disabilities.

Crooked finger, rotten bole, under stars, over soils.
The I in my old poems is no longer me. The one
in this one will be someone else soon.

Ricardo's Lunch

5th Ave. was shoulder to shoulder with
hungry lunch-seeking business men
and women. Ricardo unpacked
his horn nervously and a foot cymbal.
Spring, early street season, too cold
for most musicians but he needed money.
His lips kissed the cold metal mouthpiece.

Carrying the saw and the pulaski.
Cutting brush for a fire line high up,
where raptors and ravens fly. No sound
but wind if you could subtract the crew
working and dirty, joking during lunch.
A good year it had been sitting in the soil
feeling Ricardo's body on the mountainside.
Mountains moving as good a feeling.

Alone in his town, most neighbors at work,
housecleaning done, Ricardo settled down
with pen to write and ate lunch.
       People = chickadees.
       Clutch size, substrate, territory, gestation period.
       Mating rituals. Use of alcohol and hallucinogens.
       Forms of cancer, heart disease. Burial rites, memories.
       Creation myths, beliefs for which there is no evidence.
       Range: tundra to tropics.

KOBINA WRIGHT

Ujima

Mom:

Let me get your car keys from you.
Go get it washed, fill up the tank
hang a spearmint tree.
Come by tomorrow to help with the lawn
if you want.
Alright with groceries?

Dad:

What are you doing tomorrow?
Lunch is on me.
Want me to ride with
to your doctor's appointment?
No trouble.

Brother:

About that job I spoke to you about the other day.
Still interested?
Wrote a couple of letters on your behalf.
Hope you don't mind.
The way you're being treated ain't right.
Got you.

Sister:

Always good to see you.
Should drop by for dinner this weekend.
Bring your babies.
Were you still interested in investing?
Talk about it this weekend.
Come by early if you can.

Ujamaa

In this, our minds stand ajar
pausing, acknowledging the ring
that vibrates to our bones.
We pay ourselves in gold and silver
in contributions to our 401K
in a separate account in a credit union
in a white envelope in a book safe.
After we pay our mortgages, our rents
our car notes, utilities, child support
after our medical, phone, internet,
contractual agreements,
we show our teeth
and recycle.

It moves over us like mist in a drying sun
extracted from salt
rising as vapors, collecting overhead
growing heavy with power
pouring over us to clear
the air, engorge roots
in the saturated earth replenishing
the reservoirs so they don't
stink, wither into raisins.
When these are no longer heavy
they wisp away on wind to
cycle somewhere else.

Our water, pours down on us.
Wallets have gotten
too fat to hold the notes, the cards.
The minds are cleansed with knowledge
of love, support, heritage
engorged in the saturated loyalty of the people
replenishing our trust in each other.
We don't stink of apathy.
We don't wither.

Nia

This is not about fixing, it's about building.
Not from scraps either because we curated the
building materials conscientiously.

We put on work clothes (the clean ones—
the ones that made us feel good about the coming undertakings).
We put on our work boots to protect ourselves
from projection unseen from weightiness we may
accidentally drop on us. And gloves.
We know how delicate we really are.

We will lay out plans and review them before we
begin to erect the addition (yes, addition—we've been
here 400 years, you didn't think we were
starting from scratch…)

On this level we've decided to include additional doors, perhaps
twice as many as the level below, twice as many windows
and a sun roof for light.

We've studied the previous plans, previous construction.
Some worked. Some didn't.
Fixing comes later
after this level is halfway completed.

We've drawn no pictures for public viewing.
It's proprietary.
So no—they can't see it right now.
No, we won't feel sorry about it.

SHORT STORIES

DREADFUL AWAKENING

John W. Dennehy

The search for the bloody knife took place on a chilly day. And young Charlie's discovery turned out to be a serendipitous find, leaving him with many questions.

A fall morning, Charlie had awoken, and clambered down from the bunk bed. His frayed pajamas warded off the cold. The picture of Flash had peeled, revealing yellow, cotton beneath. He'd gotten them a couple years beforehand in '72 when the Oakland Athletics won the World Series. Padding across the unfinished floor, he headed downstairs.

The cluttered old house was quiet.

His brother and most of the children had already left for grade school. This left little Marky and the girl, Kerry. A toddler and a girl not old enough for kindergarten.

Charlie eased by the downstairs bedroom. Peering through strands of beads, he glanced into the dim room, spying a large lump under the covers. Liz lay there, still. Asleep. He feared creaking the floor.

She'd wake and punish him for the transgression.

He entered the kitchen without making too much noise. Charlie opened the cupboard and reached for a bowl. He set it on the counter, and then trundled over to the pantry and opened the door.

A large box of Kix cereal sat on the shelf.

Charlie grabbed the massive, orange box in both hands, and gently pulled it down, careful not to knock anything over. Holding the cereal box in both hands, he perused the rest of the shelf: Honeycomb, Count Chocula, and Fruity Pebbles.

He listened for the sound of footsteps. Nothing.

Kerry was likely still asleep, so he could eat peacefully, alone.

Maybe he'd eat fast enough so they wouldn't know. Charlie considered grabbing the Count Chocula, but he thought better of it. Someone might walk in and catch him. The infraction would result in severe punishment.

He would get the paddle for it.

Liz bought lots of Bo-Lo Bouncers at the discount store on Route 1 near the disco, paddle boards with a rubber ball attached by an elastic string. Charlie thought about how fun they'd been at first. When he'd first come to Liz's house, he enjoyed playing alone with them, bouncing the rubber ball off the paddle, trying to see how many times he could keep it going.

The kids that had lived there for a while never used them, so he could always find one and play for hours. Occasionally, he came across paddles with the elastic strings cut off; he'd snatch up a paddle and try to play the game without the rubber ball tethered to it. It always bounced wildly, so he could only get a few hits in before the ball shot out of reach.

Later, he realized why so many paddles didn't have strings. She'd cut them off and used the paddles to spank the kids, especially the boarders and foster children. The foster kids got the worst of it because they didn't have any parents checking up on them.

Liz's children only got beaten when they really upset her. She had already broken a few paddles on Charlie, even for things he hadn't done. He got blamed for infractions and misconduct that Liz's kids had committed. It wasn't fair.

Charlie glanced at the good cereal wondering if it was worth the risk.

Staring at the boxes, his mouth began to water. Appetite whet, he reached for the Fruity Pebbles, thinking nobody would notice some of it missing. Charlie trundled toward the breakfast counter, uncertain if he'd go through with it.

He set both boxes down on the counter, and then fetched the bowl. Charlie placed it next to the boxes and walked over to the refrigerator.

Opening the big door, he glanced inside at two cartons of milk: one for Liz and her kids, and another for everyone else. The bad milk. Always tasted sour. Sometimes the bad milk caused his stomach to hurt.

Charlie listened carefully for Liz, then grabbed the carton of good milk.

He hustled to the breakfast counter. A thud reverberated from the milk carton hitting the Formica. Charlie quickly opened the Fruity Pebbles. The plastic bag inside the box crinkled loudly. He cringed at the sound, worried it would stir Liz awake. Nothing. Then, he poured the flakes into the bowl, hands trembling.

His heart raced. Fear of getting caught.

Charlie huffed for breath.

He paused to listen.

Still nothing.

Dumping Kix cereal on top of the Fruity Pebbles, he concealed the misdeed. He poured cold milk on top. Charlie's stomach churned in anticipation.

He quickly put the milk away and stashed the Fruity Pebbles in the pantry. Sitting on a stool, he spooned the good cereal from the bottom of the bowl, soaked in fresh milk. The cereal tasted incredible. With the good milk, it wouldn't hurt his stomach, either.

Charlie greedily wolfed down the sugary cereal.

Using his spoon, he created a hole in the Kix, trying to access more Fruity Pebbles, but found nothing but milk in the bottom of the bowl. Pressing the balls of starch away, here and there, the Kix floated back into place.

He crunched some of the tasteless balls, thinking it was peaceful without the other kids, but the solitude had grown wearisome. Charlie wished he could run off to school with the other kids, catch the bus, and skip through puddles. Old enough for kindergarten, but he didn't get signed up during the shuffle into the boarding home.

A creak on the floor caused him to spin around.

Liz stood in the doorway, staring at him suspiciously. She looked haggard. Puffy eyes and short hair unkempt. The terrycloth bathrobe draped loosely, and her fleshy chest heaved with each breath, partially exposed.

The silence was dreadful.

He nervously watched her peruse the kitchen, eyeing the box of cereal and bowl on the counter. Charlie readied himself for an outburst.

"What are you doing?" she snapped.

"Eating breakfast."

"You using my milk?"

"No." His voice cracked.

Liz shuffled over, looking more drained than usual. Sniffed the bowl.

She knows our milk is bad, he thought. "Honest, I didn't…"

"I'll bet," she said, cuffing him upside the head.

Charlie reached up, feeling the welt.

"Tell your parents, and it will only get worse." She pointed to the barber shop strap hanging by the stove. A shiny liquor bottle sat on the counter near the peg where it hung. There was a red label on the front. Vodka. Somehow, he knew it was Vodka even though he couldn't read very well. Half empty.

"I won't tell, honest."

"You do… and it will only get worse. Much worse."

"We won't tell, honest. Tell 'em it's great here."

"I expect that you won't. You think they care about you… your parents?" She scowled. "They pay me to let you and your brother live here. Not enough money for you to eat up the profits on groceries, though. You got it?"

Charlie nodded, not quite understanding.

She turned away.

He watched her open the refrigerator, leaning in so her backside obscured the contents. And that was it, the end of her inquiry. Liz usually grilled him, screaming. Her eyes bugged out, and the tendons in her neck, bulging, like metal strands on a suspension bridge. The abuse directed at him often for the mistakes of others: broken toys, crumbs on the counter. Blows from her rage often knocked him to the floor.

She stood up and took a long guzzle of orange juice from the carton. Charlie and the others weren't allowed to drink the juice, only tap water. Liz moved slowly.

He'd awoken in the night to voices downstairs. A man's voice, and the sound of her teenage son, Nick.

Liz seemed drained, lethargic.

Something had happened. Her son smoked cigarettes and snuck glassfuls of liquor up to his room. The kid was a juvenile delinquent, like his older sister used to call Mike Hogan back in the old neighborhood. Hogan climbed on the roofs of cars and jumped on the hoods, denting them. He broke windows and mirrors, got in fights, and stole from the five and dime store.

Liz stepped to the sink, wearily. Something had gone wrong.

The plastic container on the windowsill had been moved.

He noticed her staring at the pill bottle. It was usually to the right, but now stood on the edge of the sill, toward the center. The bottle held her big pills. Horse pills. Valium. Charlie remembered her daughters talking about them.

Liz took the pills when she got upset.

He figured she'd taken one that night. Made her tired, dragging. Too exhausted to punish him. She stepped from the room and he breathed more easily.

Charlie put the box of Kix away. Then, he cleaned out his bowl and spoon, dried them off, and returned them to the cupboard.

He left the kitchen to go back up to his room. Stepping by the downstairs bedroom, he peered through the beads. She didn't have a door. Liz lay in a heap on the bed, breathing heavily. Wigs lined her dresser, blonde, black, brunette, and auburn. Each wig was carefully placed over a Styrofoam mannequin head.

She wore them out to local bars and brought strange men home at night.

***

Upstairs, he broke out the plastic bin that held his toy soldiers. Charlie set up the grey Germans and green Army figures, acting out pretend battles. He heard Kerry and Marky get up. They went downstairs to eat the good cereal with fresh milk, with no fear of reprisal.

Then he heard heavy footsteps on the stairs.

A chill ran down his spine.

Liz approached.

She was coming upstairs, and he was the only one there. Now, she would scream at him for using the good milk. Maybe belt him, or she'd spank him with a paddle.

The footsteps moved slowly down the hall, creaking the unfinished boards. Most of the upstairs had been torn apart for a remodel job abandoned halfway through. Nick's room was the only complete room up there. He had paneling and carpeting.

The advance ceased at the threshold to the room that Charlie shared with his brother.

Pretending not to hear, Charlie didn't look up, and made as though the toy soldiers had him engrossed, so he didn't know anyone was there.

He expected a harsh voice. And pictured her with a paddle in hand, waiting to pounce.

"Charlie…" The tone was weak, vulnerable.

He looked up.

"I *need* your help."

Charlie nodded, acknowledging.

"I understand there is a… a knife… down by the bus stop." She paused, almost as if trying to figure out what to say. "We need to go down there and find it, so no one gets hurt."

He nodded again, signaling an agreement to help.

"Come on, then," she said. "Let's get going." She turned and left.

Charlie put on a pair of ripped jeans and a t-shirt. The jeans were not meant to be stylish; holes exposed his knees from wear, and there wasn't money to buy a new pair.

He headed downstairs and found his coat in the back hallway. A windbreaker with racing stripes down the sleeves. Liz walked to the closet and put on a heavy coat, imitation fur lining in a leopard print. Surprisingly, she didn't have a wig on. Charlie had never seen her tongue tied before, and she never went out without a wig, even to the grocery store.

"Kerry will be joining us," she said.

They went to the back door, stepping outside into a chilly fall day. By the time they descended the concrete steps to the broken walkway, the girl came out and shut the door behind her.

She smiled at Charlie, skipping to catch up. Kerry wore a heavy coat too.

He could already feel the breeze whip through his light windbreaker. Charlie shivered and wished he had a winter coat, but his was too small and they hadn't gone fall shopping yet. New clothes came just twice a year.

The three of them headed through the neighborhood, down the road, full of pot holes and patches of sand and dirt. It was quite a walk to the bus stop. Dilapidated houses lined the street, abutting industrial areas. Beyond the backyards lay parking lots, and not far away, cars and trucks buzzed along Route 1, a divided highway.

Trevor, a neighborhood kid the same age as Kerry was playing outside of his house, alone. "What are you up to?" Trevor called to Charlie.

"We're on our way to look for a knife."

"Shush…" Liz snapped.

Charlie shrugged, not sure what he said wrong.

"Some older boys left a knife down by the bus stop," Liz said. "We are going to look for it, so nobody gets hurt."

Charlie didn't understand how Liz had come by this information. He expected that Nick had told her, but adults often knew things kids didn't. They sometimes got telephone calls from friends and neighbors.

"Do you want to join us?" Liz asked.

Trevor nodded, and Charlie's stomach sank. He wanted to be the one to find the knife, and he would be the hero while the big kids were off at school. But it was too late. Trevor ran to join them smiling at the prospect of an adventure.

Charlie knew the way the kids took to school. The road led to an intersecting street, and it connected to a major road. A plaza with a supermarket was down an embankment on the other side of the road, and a large median lay in the center of the busy streets.

When they got near the intersection, Charlie looked toward the bus stop. A large rock jutted near the corner of the roads. He pictured Nick waiting for the bus, smoking a cigarette behind the rock. The spot where the kids waited was loose dirt and littered with wrappers.

He ran ahead toward the bus stop.

"Stop right there," Liz called out to him.

He'd gotten twenty feet ahead of them.

"Charlie! You stop right now."

"I wouldn't run into the road," he said, slowing down.

They closed the distance, but he kept walking to reach the bus stop first. Charlie immediately searched around the big rock. He imagined the knife behind it. Bad kids hung out there, smoking and swearing, while they waited to catch the school bus. His father had warned the boys to stay away from the bus stop at night, telling them older boys drank booze by the rock.

When Liz and the others caught up, she walked by and stood at the edge of the road. "We have to go over there," she said, pointing.

A grassy area divided the major roadway. Oak trees stood in the middle of the median and shrubbery grew around them. Most of it was flat and covered in grass. The entire area was lined in granite curbing.

Charlie understood it was a traffic island.

"But the bus stop is over here," Charlie reasoned.

"Come, let's cross the street," she said.

Her tone was nice, and she reached for Kerry and Trevor's hands. Charlie trundled up beside them, and then they all raced across the street. Safely on the other side, the children frantically searched for the dangerous knife.

They circled the oak trees like running around a maypole, but the knife seemed to elude them, camouflaged by the dried grass, or maybe it wasn't there.

Liz stood by watching them nervously.

She seemed preoccupied and didn't partake in the search. Charlie wondered what had her so worried and why she didn't help look for the knife.

Trevor scrambled fervently looking for it. He didn't seem to notice Liz or pay any mind to the others. Fixated. His eyes were glued to the grass, scampering around like a hound dog with its nose to the ground. Soon enough he shot up with something in his hand.

A leather sheath.

It flapped in the boy's hand. Empty.

Trevor ran to Liz.

She praised him, but the search wasn't over. Charlie watched her put the sheath in her coat pocket. "Keep looking," she said.

He decided to move away from the others, who focused on the area around the trees. Charlie wandered over toward the far side of the median. Downhill, he noticed the roof of the grocery store, jutting above the roadway.

Then, he looked down at the ground, and saw it plain as day.

The knife lay stranded in the grass. A dirty blade and black handle.

A buck knife. His pulse raced with excitement.

Charlie moved toward it swiftly. He snatched up the knife by the handle and jogged toward Liz. "I found it!"

The others converged, desperate to get a glimpse of the knife. Defeat in their eyes.

He recognized the kind of knife it was right away. There were pictures of them in his Dad's hunting magazines, from when he lived with his parents, back before the separation. A hunting knife. It had a five-inch blade and four-inch handle. The end of the handle was shiny metal like the blade. The handle itself was ringed in black and grey bands.

Liz took the knife.

She shoved it into her purse.

A smile of relief crossed her face.

She thanked him in the kindest way. Liz had never been nice to Charlie since he started living there, always upset, and preoccupied with punishing the children.

They headed across the busy street, Liz holding the hands of the younger children; Charlie made the trek alone. He felt like a big kid, crossing the street by himself.

***

The walk took some time. Each kid ran back and forth over the desolate street, while Liz walked in silence, morose. Partway home, she abruptly stopped by a wooded area. A small track of land ran along an easement for power lines.

"We need to get rid of this knife," she said. "So... no one gets hurt."

"Can't we just throw it in the trash when we get home?" Charlie said.

"No!" She snapped, shaking her head. "Someone could get hurt reaching into the trash."

"Yeah. Someone could get hurt by it," Kerry added.

Charlie pictured the knife in the trash; the plastic bag being pulled from the can, and then the knife poking through, cutting into someone's leg. He shrugged.

"Are you going to help me, Charlie?" Liz sounded vulnerable again.

He nodded. "So, what are we going to do?"

"Follow me."

Then, Liz headed into the wooded area. She kicked up dead leaves, dragging her feet. Charlie walked behind her, and the others tagged along further back. He noticed a stream bubbling, white choppy water, traveling fast, bumping off rocks.

She pointed. The brook made a sharp turn under a small culvert.

"There!" Liz pointed at the culvert. She forged her way through brush; the kids followed suit. Stopping near the culvert, she directed Charlie to stand by the mouth, and then she took the knife from her purse.

Charlie waited patiently, wondering what she planned to do.

"Here, Charlie," she finally said, handing him the knife.

He took it carefully by the handle.

"Now, toss it in there. Way back where nobody will find it."

Charlie wound up ready to chuck the knife.

"Make sure it gets far back there, Charlie," she said, almost pleading.

His right shoulder bumped up against the culvert, impeding his throwing arm. Charlie held the knife in his left hand, worried he couldn't throw it very far.

"You can do it," Liz assured him.

Charlie pulled his arm back, then whipped the knife, sidearm, like skipping a rock. It shot into the darkness, clanging on craggy rocks lining the culvert.

"Good job, Charlie." She sounded relieved.

He watched the bubbling water cascade along. The knife had made it halfway through, landing between rocks. Out of sight. Wedged in there, so nobody would ever find it, and couldn't get hurt by the knife.

"Let's go," Liz said, gently pulling his shoulder.

He turned away from the brook and followed the others back to the road. Charlie felt like he'd accomplished something.

"I can't wait to tell the big kids," Charlie said.

"None of you should talk about this to the other kids," Liz said. "You shouldn't mention it to anyone."

"Why not?" This from Trevor.

"They might get curious. Go looking for it. Somebody could get hurt."

Trevor nodded, agreeing with her.

They walked toward Liz's house quietly, not saying a word. Charlie glanced at her and noticed how sad she looked. A tear ran from the corner of her eye.

"Why are you crying?" Charlie asked.

"It's just the wind," she said, wiping at her face. But he knew better. Something was seriously wrong. He couldn't understand why she wasn't happier, now that the knife was out of harm's way.

When the older kids got home, Charlie didn't mention the episode to them. At bedtime, he lay in the top bunk and whispered about the knife to his brother. He got excited telling the story, reliving crossing the busy road on his own, and the find.

His brother didn't respond with elation. For a moment, Charlie wondered if he'd fallen asleep listening to the story.

"Are you awake?" Charlie finally said.

"Yeah, I'm awake." His brother sounded annoyed.

"What do you think?"

"I think that you should get your rest."

Maybe you had to be there, Charlie thought.

He rolled over and took a long time to get to sleep. Kerry and Trevor must have thought he was cool, finding the knife, and being the one to toss it into the culvert.

Next morning, he went downstairs with his brother for breakfast.

He learned that Liz's oldest son Nick was gone. He'd left in the night to go stay with his father for a while. All the other big kids went off to school for the last day of the week. Charlie stayed in the house and played, and Liz was unusually nice to him.

On Saturday, their father came and picked up Charlie and his brother. They loaded into the big '71 Ford Torino. His brother sat in the front, and Charlie climbed in back and slid behind his father.

They drove out of the rundown neighborhood, retracing the steps that Charlie and the crew had taken a few days beforehand. He glanced out the window and saw the tract of land and the brook; a nub of the culvert came into view.

As they continued, the car drove past the bus stop, and then cut around the median. Charlie looked at the big oak trees, remembering the kids scurrying around them.

Then he peered out the window toward the spot where he'd found the knife.

Almost as though reading his mind, his father glanced at the median. "A kid got stabbed there the other night," he said. "High school boys... out drinking and causing trouble. Leads to no good."

Charlie gulped at the comment.

Remembering the knife when he found it, he'd caught a glimpse of the blade. And he noticed it again before he tossed it under the culvert. The dark spots on the blade weren't dirt or dried blood from a deer, but rather human blood.

Charlie didn't expect to ever see Nick again. His stomach sank, and his heart raced.

FRANNIE POTTER

Alan Fleishman

LA MANCHA

In 1937 I went to Spain to save the Republic and keep my friend Marty alive.

A small band of us arrived in Albacete on a rickety train after days on the sea, hours in the back of a bouncing truck from Paris to the French border, and a numbing climb by foot over the Pyrenees in the dark of a freezing April night to avoid French border patrols. Marty and I were here on the brown plain of La Mancha to join the Abraham Lincoln Brigade in a just and important cause.

After all that, the man in the uniform seated at the field desk in front of me insisted women couldn't fight. He said I could be an ambulance driver, cook, or nurse's aide changing bedpans and bandages.

"No sir," I answered, staring straight ahead like a soldier. "I came here to fight."

"They must have explained to you before you left America," the man in the uniform said.

"I know how to fire a gun," I lied. "And I can clobber any man here with my fists." That part was probably true. I was bigger and stronger than most of them, with broader shoulders but fewer curves than most girls. Back home I usually covered myself in pants and men's shirts, and when we reached Paris, I had my mousy brown hair cut short as a guy's.

I stared at the man behind the desk and he stared back at me, his pencil suspended over the log of new recruits. A barrel-chested man in a brown officer's uniform and black riding boots, who had been watching from nearby, came up behind him and whispered in his ear. Then he moved on. The red star on his field hat identified him as a Russian. The man behind the desk nodded and made a mark in his log. "Alright, Potter," he said. "You're in A Company."

Marty struggled down the dusty street toward the granary, our temporary home for the next nine days, weighed down with the full knapsack, uniform, and bedroll we'd each been issued. He was a small man who couldn't have stood more than five feet four or weighted more than a hundred twenty pounds even with rocks in his pockets. About halfway there I asked him to pause so I could catch my breath, really an excuse to give him a break.

He lit a cigarette. "You shouldn't have insisted on carrying a rifle, Frannie," he said.

"That's why I came," I answered. "To fight."

"Well, I'm not going to be able to take care of you once we come under fire."

"So who asked you to?" I shot back. I was the one, after all, who was there to take care of him.

He snuffed out his cigarette, and we continued walking toward the old granary, joining the other nine new recruits. We changed into our uniforms—brown flannel shirts, khaki trousers, and v-shaped caps. Marty turned his head away, too embarrassed to see me stripped down to my drawers. He would have liked to throw a blanket over me to shield me from the eyes of the other men. None of them paid any attention. I was just another soldier in the group: four pale Jews from New York City, a Negro truck driver from Chicago, a sharecropper from Tennessee, a union organizer from Cleveland, a bank clerk from Buffalo, a coal miner from Pennsylvania, Marty, and me. None of us had yet reached our twenty-fifth birthday.

That evening the two of us sat by ourselves under a Linden tree eating our plates of beans and bread with carrots and onions fried in olive oil.

"That's not thunder you're hearing," Marty said. "It's artillery fire."

"Are you glad you came?" I asked.

"You know why I came." He gave me that adorable puppy dog look that made me wonder why I couldn't love him the way he wanted me to love me. Instead, he made me feel guilty all over again.

Marty was cute as could be, but it was his brain that fascinated me right from the start. The first time we met, I thought he had his eye on my best friend, Dolores Brown. We were just starting our second year at San Francisco State College, rare for a girl, and even rarer for a desperately poor longshoreman's daughter. State was possible if I worked part-time. I wanted something more than my mother's dull, desperate life of survival. I wanted to roam the world and achieve some great purpose. Every day when I entered campus through the big door on Haight Street, I felt I moved one step closer to escaping Rincon Hill. That's where we lived, in a rundown, weathered-gray clapboard house not far from the Embarcadero where Daddy worked on the wharves.

Dolores lived down the street from us in a house no better than mine. We had been best friends for as long as I could remember, joined at the hip, my mother used to say. On the opening day of the fall semester in 1936, We headed into our first class and found seats toward the front.

Doctor Jefferson Drummond looked the part of a history professor: middle-aged, pipe smoking, thinning blondish hair, and a sonorous voice. Everyone said he was a socialist at best, and maybe even a Communist. "Who knows what's going on in Spain right now?" he challenged before everyone was even seated. Twenty-three sets of eyeballs stared at their shoes, praying he wouldn't call on them. He waited and waited some more. No one replied. I wondered if I was the only one sweating.

When all seemed lost, one voice spoke from two rows behind me. "Spain became a republic in 1931 when the people threw out their king. Then the election this past April was won by a coalition of republicans, socialists, Communists, workers, and peasants. That threatened the old order of generals, large landowners, and the Catholic Church." I turned around to see this adorable little teddy bear taking control. I later learned his name was Marty Hornstein.

"Go on," Drummond encouraged.

Marty explained that in July fascist generals led by Francisco Franco launched a civil war against the elected Republican government. Hitler immediately sent German-manned bombers, fighter planes, and transports to help Franco, along with many of their newest tanks and armaments. Mussolini did the same. Great Britain, the United States, France, and the other western democracies refused to help the elected government, their excuse being that this was an internal Spanish matter. The Russians snuck some antiquated equipment through the Italian naval blockade to the Republicans but not enough to be decisive.

After class, I caught up with Marty in the quadrangle and thanked him for saving the rest of us from humiliation. Dolores, a petite blondish temptress, immediately gave him her coy, pinky-in-the-mouth come-on. She knew how to flirt with guys. Me, I was nineteen and had yet to have my first date.

I asked Marty a couple of questions about Spain. He asked my opinion about the war and nodded his head in approval when I let him know that any side Hitler was on I was on the other. He finally glanced at Dolores and invited us both to continue the conversation over coffee in the school cafeteria. We accepted. I didn't even think about it, but if I had, I would have assumed Marty's only interest in me was to get to Dolores. That's the way it always worked before.

During the weeks that followed, Professor Drummond's lectures concentrated on the war in Spain. Nationalist forces under Generalissimo Franco took Toledo from the loyalist Republicans and closed in on Spain's capital of Madrid. Untrained Republican rag-tag militias held out. By now, I was a committed Republican, ready to back Spain's cause.

Marty, Dolores and I met nearly every day for coffee. We followed the war and commiserated over the Republicans' desperate plight. Then Dolores, receiving little of Marty's attention, became a less frequent member of our little group.

The two of us must have been a strange sight walking across campus, this monster of a girl in second-hand clothes alongside a fragile, collegiate young man in his natty sweater vest, bow tie, and gorgeous curly black hair. I didn't think much about it. We were buddies and that's all that mattered. Marty was a Jew, so I never mentioned him to Daddy and Mother. Daddy didn't like Jews much. I had never known one before Marty, and it didn't matter to me. I wasn't about to ask him over to the house anyway. I didn't want him to see where I lived.

One day, Marty asked me to a movie. "A Farewell to Arms," he said. "Gary Cooper and Helen Hayes. You'll love it." I paused, confused. Marty was a friend, my little teddy bear. For a moment I thought he might have something else in mind, like a date. When he saw the look on my face, his natural grin shriveled into a bruised smile. "You can bring Dolores," he said without enthusiasm.

Our day at the movies was months ago, and in a place as different from Albacete as Oz and Kansas. The enormity of what I was doing didn't fully bite me until my first full day as a soldier. The brigade quartermaster issued us each a rifle and a bandoleer containing a hundred cartridges. We only simulated firing. There wasn't enough ammunition to spare for the real thing. During our nine days of training, we learned to march and to follow simple commands in English and Spanish. None of us questioned the adequacy of our preparation for battle against a professional army.

Camila Castillo, our Spanish company cook, adopted me right from the start. I needed it. She had a thin black brush above her upper lip and the sagging breasts of an older woman, though she was probably no more than my mother's forty-three years. She told me, through gaps in her broken browned teeth, how to take care of a woman's needs in the field. She also warned me not to get involved with men with whom I shared the trenches. The later advice was advice I didn't need. I hadn't come to Spain to find a boyfriend. But if I had, the odds were good. There were only 80 American women among the three thousand American men in the Abraham Lincoln Brigade.

Every day we heard the booming of cannon from the front only a few miles off. Occasionally trucks carrying troops sped toward the front or returning ambulances raced toward the hospital down the street. One time a fleet of about twenty German Heinkel bombers crossed above us in the high blue sky, headed toward Madrid.

On the evening of our ninth day of training, we were fed a huge pile of Camila's chopped potatoes, vegetables, and a chewy but tasty chunk of goat spiced with garlic, peppers, and parsley. Wine flowed from the wineskins until anxiety waned. Tomorrow we were to be put to the fire.

Small wonder I couldn't sleep that night. I lay awake thinking about the first time I heard of the Abraham Lincoln Brigade when Professor Drummond brought it up in class. He told us the unit consisted of American volunteers who traveled to Spain to join in the defense of the Republic. Their gallantry helped save Madrid for the moment.

When we came out of class that day, Marty carried a printed blue flyer Drummond had handed him. JOIN THE FIGHT it said. An illustration of a muscled man, a rifle raised above his head, dominated the top of the page. It advertised a meeting to be held Thursday evening at 7:00 pm at the Workers' Hall off Van Ness Street.

"Let's go," I said impulsively.

"I'm not going to Spain," Dolores grumbled.

"Maybe we can help in some other way," Marty said. "Let's hear what they have to say."

"Okay," Dolores relented. "But I'm not going to Spain."

I was no longer so sure of that, so I kept my mouth shut.

The room was set up to hold about fifty people, but only nine showed, six young men plus Marty, Dolores and me. The small audience did not diminish the zeal of the two men up front. One was a well-spoken, modestly dressed middle-aged American in a suit. The other was a slender, handsome, mustached Spaniard in black pants and a white shirt opened at the collar. A few tufts of dark chest hair showed. He was gorgeous, and I was captured, not so much by him as with what he said.

First, the American gave a short speech about how the Republic had been democratically elected to serve the workers and peasants, and how the fascists with German and Italian help were trying to overthrow it.

Then the Spaniard rose to speak, his English fluent but with a decided accent. Dramatic gestures punctuated his every fervent word. He showed us a movie of fascist bombs destroying Spanish cities and killing innocent people. Rows of Franco's goose-stepping regular army soldiers contrasted with the brave Republican militias of armed workers and peasants. There were shots of determined Americans in the Abraham Lincoln Brigade undergoing training before moving into battle. When the film ended, the Spaniard closed with an impassioned plea for us to come to Spain to join *la causa*—the cause. "We fight not just for ourselves, but for ordinary people everywhere," he said. "*Por favor*, we cannot let democracy die, murdered by tyrants."

By the time he finished, my blood pumped like water through a fire hose. I realize now that I had been searching for a way to fight back against injustice ever since Daddy was badly beaten by police during the 1934 longshoremen's strike. How helpless he and the other workers were to resist the power of the shipowners, the mayor, the governor, the police, and the national guard arrayed against them to break the strike. Here in Spain, a whole people were going through something even worse.

Two young working men signed up immediately. The others milled around talking to the Spaniard or the American. I pulled Marty and Dolores into a corner in the back of the room.

"We've got to go," I said, about to burst.

Dolores looked at me as though I had flipped my lid. "You've got to be kidding. I'm not going to Spain, for godsake."

"Let's settle down," Marty said. "This is serious business."

"Real people are dying," I shot back. "And did you see those Americans over there ready to fight? They have courage."

Marty said nothing. Neither did Dolores. I stood there, erect as a soldier, hands on hips, my glare fixed on Marty until he looked away.

"You'd better think this over, Frannie," he finally said.

"I'm signing up right now."

He took a deep breath. "Alright. I can't let you go alone." So, the two of us signed up.

Dolores refused to speak to me all the way home until we got off the streetcar and walked the last few blocks to our neighborhood.

"If he's killed it's going to be your fault," she said, spite in her voice.

"What are you talking about?"

"Are you so blind?" She sniffled and wiped her nose on the back of her hand. "He's been sweet on you since the first day he met you. That's why he's going. For you, not for some stupid cause."

I was speechless and as blind as she said I was. Witless nineteen-year-old girls like me thought the only kind of love was the romantic love one sees in the movies. I didn't know there was any other kind. Marty and I had a special friendship, I knew that. But not a romance. Yet the moment Dolores said it I knew she was right. He was willing to risk his life because he loved me. And I couldn't return that kind of love. That's a lot of guilt for a young woman to carry around in her knapsack. But it's how we ended up in Spain together in the middle of a civil war.

Marty snored in the cot next to mine. I envied him. Tomorrow we were going to take on the fascists in battle, and I was supposed to keep Marty alive, as well as save the Spanish Republic. And the hell of it was I didn't even know how to fire a rifle.

BATTLE

The morning we were bloodied for the first time broke humid and gray. People would be killed, but I never thought I might be one of them. Our company was ordered to hold a strong point protecting Madrid against attack by a fierce force of Moroccans from the Spanish African Legion. "Stay close to me," Marty commanded when we jumped down from the back of the truck. I nodded. I had no intention of being anywhere else.

Artillery explosions shocked my eardrums and shook the ground worse than a San Francisco earthquake. Thick smoke burned my eyes and gunpowder stuffed my nostrils. The rat-a-tat-tat from a machine gun nest resounded to my right. Whatever I expected war to be, I never expected it to be so loud and haphazard.

Our group crouched behind a stone parapet in an unplowed field. A sunburned road ran down to our left. I grabbed hold of Marty's belt to make sure he was within arm's length. The menacing Moors in their terrifying turban headdress moved from one trench and hill defilade to another with well-trained precision. Our side fired and fired, but the rounds from our antiquated Russian rifles died a hundred yards out, worthless. The fascists had new, modern German *Mauser Karabiner* bolt-action rifles that can hit a man at three hundred meters. The enemy crept closer and closer with deadlier and deadlier fire. One of the Jewish kids in our group from New York fell on his back, his legs bent under him, a big messy hole in his stomach, and a surprised look on his dead face. In the confusion of their assault, I lost sight of Marty. I shouted his name but with all the noise it was like shouting into the wind on a stormy night.

One of the bearded Moors, now nearly upon us, showed himself, his black eyes fixed on me. I took careful aim and fired my rifle for the first time. He suspended in mid-stride, paused, and toppled over. I felt the exhilaration a big game hunter must feel when he bags his first lion. Then I did it again and again and again. Each time I pulled the trigger a man fell and my heart pounded in celebration.

My last round stopped one of the bearded bastards not fifty feet from our wall. His Mauser rifle lay near his outstretched hand beckoning me. I had to have it. I crawled over the wall and made a run for it. The ping-ping-ping of rounds landed near me kicking up puffs of dirt. They barely registered. I wanted that rifle. I grabbed it, yanked the cartridge belt from the dead body, and then turned and scurried back.

I was nearly over the wall when a deep burn bit my calf. I fell to safety, blood on my pants. I'd been nicked. It hurt a little, but not much - a slight tingle, followed by a little hot and a little cold. Marty crawled over and poured water on it from his dented canteen, then wrapped a gray bandage around the wound, tying it in place.

"Are you nuts?" he yelled. "You could have gotten yourself killed."

"Look at this rifle," I answered, sticking out my new weapon for him to see.

We held our own that day until three German tanks smashed into our lines. An antitank gun knocked out one of them, but the other two advanced, firing on the Spanish company on our right flank until they broke and ran. We had no choice but to withdraw and regroup on the next hill behind a clump of farmhouses. The fascists did not pursue us.

A cluster of us sprawled beneath a tree in front of the lone remaining wall of an ochre *casita* smoking those long Russian cigarettes with cardboard tips and sharing a canteen of raw red wine. An essence of bull testes swirled in the air. Men who have been in battle smell like men in heat. A woman is little better. The Soviet officer who interceded on my behalf the first day ambled over. He had the broad forehead, bushy eyebrows, and squinty eyes of a Siberian Tatar. I learned his name was Oleg Veselov, and he was a major.

"Good shoots Comrade Potter," he said in a tainted Russian accent. He nodded at my Mauser. "Nice rifle. Kill more fascists."

I saw men die that day for the first time, and I killed. None of it bothered me as long as it wasn't me who died, and it wasn't Marty. After the battle, our Spanish interpreter, Diego Valera, gave me the nickname of *la asesina*—the assassin. Everyone soon called me that except Marty. He still called me Frannie.

In the second and third battles that soon followed, I felt I wore magic armor that protected me. But by the fourth or fifth battle, I prayed to God I wouldn't be the one to die. And I didn't even believe in God. By then, I hardly paid attention when my brethren shot a few Nationalist prisoners after the fighting died down, routine vengeance repaid in kind.

During the months that followed, my muscles grew hard as a bull's behind, my skin turned the color of dark earth, and my hair bronzed under the Castilian sun. It was much the same for Marty except his black hair remained black, and he grew a handsome mustache. He looked healthy for the first time since I met him. The Spanish women of Madrid couldn't keep their eyes off him; the prostitutes would have served him for free if he were willing. At least that's what the other guys in our group teased.

We were now under an unrelenting barrage from the Nationalists' artillery. Fleets of German and Italian aircraft terror bombed civilians in the center of Madrid without letup. The Republican air force could only respond with old bi-planes, and not enough of them.

We no longer had any illusions about the limits to which Franco, Hitler, and Mussolini would go. It made me angry, but for Marty, it ignited a frightening fury and despair that had no bottom. I worried about the heedless risks he took when we got into vicious firefights with German units. After such battles, he sought out German prisoners to execute.

I wrote home to Daddy and Mother whenever I could, telling them often about the brave and noble Spanish men, women, and children I had quickly come to love. I assured them with lies that, being a woman, I was kept safely behind the lines, out of harm's way. "I'll be proud of you no matter what the result," Daddy wrote, "for standing up for the little guy." He was following the war closely, he said. Mother, on the other hand, rarely wrote, and when she did, she told me how worried she was. She reminded me of the heartache I caused by sneaking off to Spain in the middle of the night without even saying goodbye.

Marty's frequent packages from home usually contained a few luxuries and a copy of the San Francisco Chronicle. He shared his Lifebuoy soap with me, good enough to wash off some of the lice and fleas. He shared his mountain of candy with the children. I'd never seen him so happy as when he was playing with the little ones, or so sorrowful as when one of them was killed.

Late on an afternoon in early July, our battalion commander, with Soviet Major Petrov by his side, briefed us on the big offensive to begin the following morning. The Republican army, with the help of Russian military advisers, prepared to launch a surprise attack designed to relieve Nationalist pressure on Madrid and cut their lines in two.

When the briefing ended, Marty and I found a corner in a damaged church where we could bed down for the night. Marty seemed taken by our spiritual sanctuary. "I don't think I can live up to the goodness of these people we're fighting for," he said quietly, a catch in his voice.

"You? You're a Boy Scout," I laughed. "I can't imagine you doing anything worse than sneaking into a movie."

"You don't even know what I did last night," he said, dropping his gaze.

"You mean your roll with that prostitute?" I was just taking a wild guess, but Marty's mouth dropped open, embarrassed. I must admit I found it hard to picture Marty with one of those busty women with the painted lips and fake flower in her coal black hair. It didn't take much to imagine this was Marty's first time. I was peculiarly jealous, though at least if he died he wouldn't die a virgin.

"Please please," he begged. "Don't tell anyone back home."

I laughed again. "For Chrissake, Marty. What makes you think we'll even be alive by this time tomorrow?"

He averted his eyes. Then he smiled. "You're right. Still, I don't want you to think less of me."

"For being with a whore? That's what you're worried about?"

"You've done worse?"

I paused, not wanting him to think the less of me either. Then I proceeded to tell him about my favorite black and white saddle shoes I stole from the Emporium Department Store on Market Street back home.

"That's it? No wonder I love you." The adorable way he said it made me want to grab him and hug him. But soldiers don't do that the night before a big battle. I reached over and grabbed his hand tightly in mine. He gripped back and held on.

Brunete lay not more than twenty miles from Madrid's *Plaza Mayor*, but it may as well have been on the outskirts of hell. From the first day to the last, twenty in all, we baked like snakes in the sands of the Sahara. Thirst tortured us as much as Nationalist bombs and bullets.

For a change, we were the ones on the attack with tens of thousands of troops, over a hundred tanks, armored cars, and heavy artillery. Some of our equipment was new and modern, each piece bearing the red star of our Soviet benefactors. We surprised the fascists, the Abraham Lincoln Brigade once again given the honor of leading from the center of the assault. The Italian forces opposing us broke and ran.

In the first skirmish, we found a handful of our comrades who had been captured. The fascists had executed them all, but not before torturing them alive and desecrating their dead bodies in the foulest manner.

Wave after wave of our brave fighters fell in our attacks like wheat stalks before a thresher. Wildfires burned across the dry yellow hills, ignited by the artillery explosions. The sun, the heat and the smoke dried my throat to a bitter cinder; wind-blown dust caked on my nose and lips. When on the fourth day there were few of us left, we made a desperate drive on Mosquito Ridge. We mustered the strength to charge the fascist trenches only because someone said they had water. Marty and I stuck to each other like salami and cheese.

A few of us fought our way to one of their bunkers. I threw a grenade into the slit killing everyone inside. A survivor in the trench outside raised his hands in surrender. I saw two canteens dangling from his belt, so I raised my Mauser rifle and fired three shots into his belly, relishing the terror in his face. He dropped. Marty watched, his lips grizzled as the grim reaper, then raised his rifle and fired three more shots into his face, demolishing his expression. We took the dead man's canteens and paused long enough for a couple of good slurps of warm water. By then the assault had stalled. Our dead comrades lay in piles.

Things didn't go well after that. Many more Nationalist troops and those from the German Condor Legion poured into the battle. High above, the German fighter planes knocked our outnumbered, outmoded planes from the sky. After nearly three weeks of hell, both sides ceased major operations. Every one of the original eleven in our group was dead except Marty, me, and the son of the kosher butcher from Brooklyn.

In the following months, the Republicans lost vital battles at Bilbao, Zaragoza, and Gijon in the north. As the year of 1937 drew to a close, many of the Abraham Lincoln Brigade survivors were ready to go home. Not me. And as long as I stayed, Marty stayed. I wish he hadn't.

By now I was so much the soldier that I could have forgotten I was a woman except for the sex. It was an available, uncomplicated diversion. I found I quite enjoyed it and maybe was even good at it. With so few American women in the country, I was a unique commodity, a curiosity if nothing else. I had never even spoken to a Negro man before I left home. Then I let a Negro man have me, in just the way you think. His name was Luther Hodges, the first man I ever slept with. After that came a Polish volunteer, and then a Spanish anarchist from

Valencia. He smelled like a pig sty with onion breath strong enough to kill a bull. But I liked him. I didn't get around to a normal white American Christian until near the end.

Sex with Marty was out of the question. You see, I wanted his respect more than I wanted the respect of any person alive. In those last few months, Marty and I shared everything: our food, our ammunition, and even our underwear. We shared our most awful secrets, our brightest hopes, and our passion for the Spanish people. We convinced each other we were going to survive this.

HEADQUARTERS

For the first two months of 1938, we battled on bravely winning a small victory here and there only to be crushed in the end by overwhelming Nationalist counterattacks. We lost more people. We retreated. Franco's army kept attacking, giving us no rest. By mid-April they reached the Mediterranean Sea, cutting the Republic in half. The remnants of our brigade withdrew into the collapsing Catalonian pocket.

Marty hadn't smiled in weeks, his good nature replaced by sacrilegious sarcasm. A leather wine bag tucked in his knapsack was now a constant temptress. We continued to eat together and sleep next to each other, but he rarely talked to me or anyone, his eyes hollow and his face a milky gray. In the next battle, and the two after that, he took reckless chances, daring the fates or fascists to kill him. I didn't know how I was going to keep him alive if he didn't want to stay alive. Then the devil took a hand.

This one particular afternoon in August, our trucks unloaded us in a small farm town a hundred miles to the west of Barcelona. Its one paved street ran down to a narrow wooden bridge over the Ebro River. Our group found a spot in the dark barren cellar of a pock-marked two-story building.

Marty and I slung our knapsacks and rifles to the floor, exhausted. He set to cleaning his rifle and sharpening his bayonet, his dry, cracked lips fixed in a stony grimace. I pulled a stale piece of bread from my pack and offered half to him. He shoved it in his mouth and took a squirt of wine. "Enough of the wine," I said, perhaps a little too sharply.

He glared at me through red-veined eyes. "They're going to hunt us down and kill us all," he snarled. "Even the Russians are bugging out."

"No, they're not," I responded. "I just saw Major Veselov."

Every muscle in Marty's body tensed, resenting the increased attention the Russian was paying me. "It's time we went home," he said.

"You go home," I answered. Then I said it again, quietly. "Please. Go home."

"Come with me."

"I can't."

He lifted his wine bag above his head again and squirted a long stream down his throat. About then our company commander descended the open wooden steps and called my name. "Potter. Can you run these dispatches up to battalion headquarters?" he asked.

"Yes, sir." I leaped to my feet, glad to be out in the air and away from my morose friend for a while.

The battalion staff always picked a nice *palacio* for its headquarters. I delivered the leather pouch with the dispatches to a lieutenant and then lingered around chatting, trying to pick up the latest gossip. They didn't know any more than I did. I was about to leave when my old friend, and I use that word loosely, Major Oleg Veselov entered through the front door.

"Ah, Comrade Potter. You are still with us."

"By luck," I smiled.

"And your friend?" he asked, referring to Marty.

"Still here."

"Such a pity," he said, suggesting other possibilities if Marty were gone. He smiled in the tortured way Russians did when they tried to cover their insincerity. He paused a moment, and then touched my face. "*Hermosa*," he said. Beautiful. His Spanish had improved a little, but not his bullshit.

An unlikely thought crossed my mind. "Major. I need a favor. A big favor. Not for me. For my friend Marty Hornstein. He is not well, but he insists on fighting the next fight. If he does, he will die."

"And what would you ask of me?"

"Assign him to the battalion staff. Away from the fighting. Just for a little while. Until he gets well." I was begging and I knew it, but I had no choice.

"And what do you have to offer for such a favor?" He put one hand in his pocket and one on his hip, examining me up and down.

"What can I offer?" I asked. "I have nothing but what you see."

"*Mujer*. That is enough."

He had called me a woman, though I looked like a dead rat and smelled like one, my hair in tangles, and my dust-covered uniform in tatters. I couldn't believe what I had to offer could pay for what I was asking. He seemed to think it did.

We went down a hallway to a room in the rear of the house, a single bed with a filthy mattress in the corner. The major unfastened his high buttoned tunic deliberately and dropped his pants. It didn't take him long to finish. He seemed as satisfied with our bargain as I was. He even tried to be a gentleman, not the usual Russian brute. True to his word, he immediately sent orders for Marty to report to headquarters. Then the major treated me to some Russian honey cake. He said his mother had sent it, but I suspect it was his wife. I savored the cake, chewing each bite slowly.

Ten minutes later, I was on my way out the door. The street was oddly quiet and still. My boots thudded on the dusty cobblestones, grating on a sore spot outside my little toe. The major's smell floated from my body and into my nose. Halfway back to the company, Marty trudged toward me up the middle of the street, his knapsack, bedroll, and rifle slung over his sagging back. When he saw me, his face twisted into a scowl. I stopped, my arms outstretched to him.

"You whore," he growled when he was nearly upon me. "Who asked you to butt in?"

My heart sank when I realized my sacrifice earned me no grace. "Marty, please," I pleaded.

He brushed past me and kept walking.

I turned to see him enter the battalion headquarters just about the time I recognized the drone of approaching German Junker bombers, many of them. Our machine guns and antiaircraft guns opened deafening fusillades from the rooftops. Still, the bombers churned toward us. I ducked in a doorway when I heard the whistles of falling bombs.

A cloud of powdered cobblestone rose in front of me with the first explosions. Another hit down the street, and another around the corner. A child screamed and then a mother. I crouched lower in the doorway but could not make myself small enough. A machine gun and antiaircraft gun ceased firing when an explosion ripped through the roof of a nearby building.

The flotilla of Junkers passed. Dust and debris covered me. I was ready to bolt when the next wave of Heinkel bombers let loose their cargoes of high explosive ordnance. I ducked in my doorway again and covered my ears.

One explosion burst close to the headquarters, a near miss. The next three were right on target, so precise and devastating the bombardiers must have known the *palacio* was the command center. Marty was in that building.

I raced down the street and through the open door. Plaster dust blew down on me. Broken glass and crumbled bricks crunched under my feet. A wall was gone and blue sky glimmered through the shattered roof. I tripped over a body. Across the room, the dead Major Veselov lay against an unscathed field desk covered with rubble. He was missing half of his head. He seemed to stare at me from his one remaining eye. The foul odor of explosives and gore churned my gut.

Other bodies scattered the room. "Marty," I screamed. "Marty." No one answered. Then from the far corner near the hallway, I heard my name called ever so faintly: "Frannie."

Marty was on his knees, his rifle by his side, blood streaming down his forehead and across his crust-covered cheek. His hands rested on his thighs. He turned and looked at me without expression or recognition. Then he toppled over.

I picked Marty up, carried him out of the building, and down the street to the medical aid station. It was like walking through the main boulevard of hell, fires burning, smoke obscuring the light of day, acrid high explosive gases choking, bodies sprawled on the cobblestones - two of them little girls holding hands. Some survivors ran, some walked like zombies. Some voices shouted commands and others pleaded for help or salvation. By now the bombers had passed. Crews rushed to rescue those from beneath the wreckage.

"Don't you die, Marty. Don't you dare die," I shrieked at him. His eyes sunk back into his head, unresponsive.

When I burst into the aid station, Marty lay lifeless in my numb arms, one dangling leg nearly severed. The big lobby of the town's only hotel churned with the dead, dying, and those trying to thwart the flow. "Help me. Help me." I screamed it over and over, hysterical, until a scrawny Spanish nurse ran over. She took one look at Marty and shook her head. "Get a doctor," I threatened, "or I'll kill you." She must have believed me because she ran off.

A red-headed doctor with an Irish brogue raced over, the scrawny Spanish nurse behind him. "Put him there," he said pointing at a blood-splattered table. I lowered Marty as gently as I could. He moaned when his dangling leg dragged on the table top.

The doctor checked his breathing with his stethoscope and shined a flashlight in his eyes. He tore away the remnants of Marty's pants leg and checked the grievous wound. "You have to save him," I demanded, my heart hammering like a cannon.

The fatigued doctor turned his burned-out blue eyes on me. "We'll try," he said. "Now go wait outside until I come and get you."

I did what he said, taking a seat on the sidewalk, my back against the wall. I smoked one cigarette after another. What I really needed was some whiskey.

It may have been an hour later, or two, or maybe only fifteen minutes when the Irish doctor came out. "He's going to live," he said. "He's a lucky fellow. You saved his life."

"Can I see him?"

"There's one more thing," the doctor continued. "We can't save the leg. We're going to evacuate him to a hospital where they can amputate it."

"Oh my god. Save me."

Marty was still unconscious when I went in to see him. The pandemonium had diminished to mere frenzy, the dead removed and the damaged placed in makeshift beds. Some of his color had returned. His head was bandaged. I held his hand and bent down and kissed him on the lips. "You deserved better than me," I whispered.

Stretcher bearers carried him out to a waiting ambulance where he was loaded on, along with two other men. The scrawny Spanish nurse climbed in behind him. They closed the doors and sped off. Marty was gone. But he was alive.

ADRIFT

A few weeks later in September of 1938, the Republic's prime minister, Juan Negrin, ordered the withdrawal of all foreign fighters from the country. He had nothing to lose, wagering the international community, through the League of Nations, would then pressure Franco to remove all German and Italian forces. Negrin lost his hollow wager. One day I was spending all I had in frantic fighting, killing all the fascists I could, my own life no longer of much importance. The next day my war ended abruptly, with a whimper, our battalion pulled out of the line.

On October 29th, the men, women and children of Barcelona gathered to bid farewell to our international brigade, volunteers who came from across the world to save their republic. War raged nearby, but it didn't stop what must have been a million people from turning out on the streets, on the balconies, and hanging out of the windows. Spanish units in their finest uniforms paraded before us, but when the crowds lining the Diagonal saw us marching by in our tattered garb, they screamed and roared like a storm sweeping down a canyon.

We marched with our heads high and our arms raised in clenched-fist salute. Mothers held up their children for us to see and to see us. One little girl with big black eyes caught mine and threw me a kiss. I smiled. Flowers carpeted the street a foot deep. Tears ran down the cheeks of my new friend, Yvette Bisset, a pretty young French-Canadian volunteer from Montreal who marched at my side. She had seen her own share of mayhem in the past year from behind the wheel of an ambulance.

When the parade was over, we were taken by bus through the terraced mountainsides to the town of Ripoll north of Barcelona, twenty-five miles from the French border. There we waited for nearly a month, the cold biting at us through dark skies. The food was meager, some of it with the odor of rot. Representatives of the U.S. government at last verified we were Americans entitled to repatriation and issued us the necessary certification. These officials considered us all Communists and were none too eager to have us back.

Still in a raw state of confused despair, I ended up in Marseilles with my new-found friend, Yvette Bisset. We rented a small, dingy flat above a rowdy bar near the docks. Rats and cats kept us company, but at least it was warm, dry, and free of gunfire.

In early February, I finally boarded a ship for America. I kept to myself during those eight days on the sea, gazing into the churning waves and mist, the skies above a grim gray. Every morning began with rage in my gut, ready to fight again. Every evening ended in dark solitude, haunted by the sad weathered brown faces of Spanish children and the piles of enemy dead. Sometimes I felt sorry for myself for still being alive, but much of the time I was too exhausted to care.

When I landed in New York, I was not yet ready to head home to San Francisco. You see, I couldn't yet face Marty. There was a lot to figure out first. So, I grabbed a train to Philadelphia, and then after a while moved on to Baltimore.

In mid-March of 1939, Hitler invaded Czechoslovakia. Two weeks later, Republican forces in Spain surrendered and the United States recognized the Franco government. A week after that, Mussolini seized Albania.

After Baltimore, came Pittsburgh, Cincinnati, and St. Louis. In each place, I looked up a few comrades from the Abraham Lincoln Brigade when I could find them, or their parents if they were dead. The grieving mothers and fathers embraced me like an unexpected visitation from the beyond. I lied to them when I told them how bravely their sons had died, and how painlessly.

On the Greyhound between Kansas City and Chicago, I started a letter to Marty. Twice before I wrote him telling him about the final months in Spain, my special feelings for him, and how sorry I was for what happened to him. But the letters sounded like self-pity so I threw them away unmailed. This one was no better. I crumpled it up and tossed it in a trash barrel during a rest stop in Springfield.

The truth was I could never give him back his leg or his soul. And I couldn't give him the kind of love he wanted. Yet I loved him deeply in my own special way, in a way maybe even better than the way he wanted me to love him. In the good times, away from battlefields, he made me happy and content, and I made him happy and content. We were best friends. What could be better than that?

In late July, a letter from Daddy caught up with me in Omaha. He simply said, *"Come home, Frannie. It's time."* The next day I bought a train ticket to San Francisco on the California Zephyr.

GUERNICA

For nearly four days, loneliness and anticipation rode with me across the prairies, across the rivers and over the Rocky Mountains, lost in thoughts of San Francisco, Mother, Daddy, my little brother Ernie—and Marty.

Again and again, I came back to Marty. Remember, this was 1939. Good Protestant girls like me didn't get mixed up with Jewish boys. Still, here was this wonderful man who loved me so much he was willing to follow me into a war. I prayed he would forgive me for everything. And if he did, what then? Life would be unimaginable without him in it.

Daddy was so glad to see me alive he would have forgiven me anything. Mother forgave nothing. She still hadn't gotten over my running off to Spain in the middle of the night without telling her. Ernie, my little brother wasn't so little anymore. His voice was changing and he was nearly as tall as me. Ernie was the only one brave enough to ask me about the white scars on my leg and my neck. No one could see the other scars with my clothes on.

For the first few days home, all I did was sleep, wallowing in the cleanliness of the bed and Mom's cooking. Meat appeared on our plates more often than before I left. Daddy twice took me to meet his buddies at the longshoremen's union hall. A few checked me out, but most treated me like a celebrity, a respected war veteran.

I was not welcomed home a hero by everyone. A couple of months earlier, while I still wandered America, the FBI rapped on our door inquiring about me. They wanted to know if I was a Communist. "She ain't here," Daddy said. "Don't live here no more. Now get off my front porch." When I heard the story, I gave him a big hug.

Coit Tower, Telegraph Hill, the Ferry Building, and the bay were more beautiful that late summer than I can ever remember. I woke each morning smelling the fog drift in. The city of San Francisco was so normal it felt oddly dull. Crowds on Market Street and Union Square went about their business without a care in the world. Daddy worked nearly every day now for good wages, and Mother no longer had to serve us watery soup. Yet everything seemed without purpose. The opening of the International Exposition on Treasure Island captured more attention than the death of democracy in Spain or Hitler's threats of war in Europe. I wondered if anyone in San Francisco was reading the newspapers.

A few weeks passed. The end of August neared and still I hadn't let Marty know I was home. I was afraid he wouldn't even see me. Fear collided with yearning. When I couldn't stand it anymore, I did what every coward does. I sought an intermediary.

My old friend Dolores Brown worked at the Rexall Drug Store on Mission Street. It was close to quitting time when I stopped in. She tried hard to act glad to see me, but she never was much of an actress. I asked her out for a cup of coffee at the big Woolworth's on Market and Powell. On our walk over, we struggled to pick up the loose thread of an old friendship. She was disinterested in my ordeal in Spain, or about much of anything of substance. She was entering her senior year at San Francisco State College. All she talked about was her dull classes and the goofy boys she hung out with. I gathered she was still a virgin, so her life couldn't have been all that thrilling.

A waitress in a pink and white uniform brought us the coffees we'd ordered. Dolores filled her cup with milk and two pounds of sugar. I took mine black as tar. I lit a cigarette, and stared off into space, my arms locked around myself.

"You're different since you're back," she said.

I didn't respond until my comprehension caught up with the sound of her voice. "What do you hear about Marty?" I asked.

"You haven't seen him yet?"

"No. Should I?"

"That might not be such a good idea," she said. "I don't think he wants to see you." Her smug look suggested she enjoyed saying it.

"How do you know that?"

"Because he told me. I saw him when we were signing up for classes. He showed me his wooden leg and said you gave it to him. He wasn't joking." Then she delivered her big shot. "He also told me he has a serious girlfriend. A Jewish girl his mother fixed him up with."

I didn't much like Dolores after that. Maybe I never did. Still, her message about Marty rang true. I could hardly blame him. Why hadn't I been able to give him the words of love he wanted to hear? That's all it would have taken.

Two days after my conversation with Dolores, I woke with a pit in my stomach, not an unusual feeling for me these days. Another nightmare must have visited me in the night. When my head cleared, I recognized the smell of bacon coming from the kitchen. The sun was up so Daddy mustn't have been going to work today. I put on my robe and went downstairs. He sat alone at the kitchen table reading the front page of the Chronicle. A dirty plate of what had been eggs and bacon sat in front of him. Smoke curled from the cigarette between his yellowed fingers. He looked up when he saw me, a troubled expression on his wrinkled face. I poured myself a cup of coffee from the metal pot sitting on the stove and sat down beside him at the table.

"Not good news this morning, Frannie," he said, handing me the newspaper.

The large headline across the front page screamed: NAZIS, SO-VIETS SIGN PACT; HITLER TELLS BRITISH IT'S TOO LATE FOR PEACE; ALL EUROPE ARMS!

I scanned the articles about the crisis. Hitler demanded Poland capitulate to German terms under threat of invasion. The British and French repeated their pledge to defend Poland and began mobilization. Roosevelt hurried back to Washington from a vacation cruise to urge peace among the belligerents.

"Where were these assholes in Spain? Hitler could have been stopped there," I fumed. Daddy cringed at my coarse language.

"This ain't your fight, Frannie," he said, gently placing his rough hand on my arm.

"I didn't know much about Hitler before Spain," I said. "I know him now. He isn't going to stop." I pulled my arm from under his hand and took a cigarette from his pack of Chesterfields.

"You're not thinking of doing something stupid, are you?"

"Stupid? You think what I did was stupid?"

"I didn't mean it that way honey." He took a last puff and snubbed out his cigarette in the metal ashtray. "It's just that I look at those scars on you and I want to weep."

I covered the white blotch on my throat with my hand. "What am I going to do? Just sit here and wait for Hitler to sail into San Francisco Bay?"

The next afternoon the mailman knocked on our front door to deliver a letter with an international postmark. "Thought it might be important," he said, tipping his hat to me. The letter was postmarked Montreal from my friend Yvette Bisset. *It's time to fight again*, she wrote.

Canada will be in it. America won't. Come join me. She signed it: *Your comrade forever, Yvette.* I stuffed the letter in my dress pocket.

That night I tossed and turned until the early hours. When I went downstairs in the morning, Mother, Daddy, and Ernie were huddled around the radio. "Warsaw is under bombardment by German Heinkel and Junker bombers," the agitated British announcer chattered. "Nazi troops and tanks crossed the border at dawn this morning at many points and are now rolling through the Polish countryside." Mother looked up at me with the long ashen face of a woman whose child is soon to be taken from her. She held Ernie's hand tightly. Daddy stared at the radio as if beaten dumb. The radio station cut to its correspondent in Berlin and then to its London correspondent where the British moved to a full war footing.

I picked up Ernie's baseball bat and would have smashed the radio with it if Ernie hadn't rushed over and thrown his arms around me. "Don't go away again," he begged. I hugged him and ran my fingers through his hair.

I needed room to breathe, away from my family. I wandered downtown. The usual Friday crowds weren't there. The few men and women I passed looked sober as morticians, hands buried in their pockets against the crisp overcast morning and the chill of war. I decided to escape to one of the bars on Market Street but none of them were open yet. In front of one of them, a huge poster advertised the exhibit of Pablo Picasso's already-famous *Guernica* at the Museum of Modern Art, the first stop on its American tour to raise money for Spanish war relief. The huge painting depicted in stark black, white, and brown the terror bombing of the town of Guernica in northern Spain during the second year of the war. Sixteen hundred women, children, and old men died helplessly in the attack.

The museum exhibiting Picasso's masterpiece was in the War Memorial Veterans Building, a short walk past city hall and across Van Ness Avenue. I pulled my coat tight around me and followed my feet without much thinking.

When I stepped off the elevator and into the room, *Guernica* surrounded me, massive, from the floor to the high ceiling. I looked but did not see Picasso's wild-eyed bull, the terrorized woman, the tortured horse, or the flame in the lamp. Instead, I saw my fallen comrade, Diego, his arm severed at the elbow, his hand still gripping his rifle. I saw a mother in front of me who died screaming in Zaragoza, with her dead baby in her arms. I saw dead Americans from my group with their guts and their brains oozing out onto the streets of Villanueva. I saw bombs from German planes exploding on innocent children and old women. And, at last, I saw Marty covered in plaster, his body limp, a leg dangling by threads. All of this at the hands of barbarians - fascists. No one came to help my noble Spaniards except those of us from the Abraham Lincoln Brigade. Now it was happening again, bombs whistling down on Warsaw in the early morning light, the Nazi blitzkrieg poised to sweep across Europe and to America. Who was going to stop them?

The room began to spin. I stumbled backward, staggered over to an oak bench in the center of the room and collapsed onto it. For the first time since Spain, tears fell in unrelenting cascades. I shook all over, as feverish as at the battle of Brunete and as frozen as at Teurel. Still, I could not take my eyes from Guernica. If anyone else was in the exhibit room, I didn't see them. I slumped over and closed my eyes against the horrors. How long I lay there on the bench, in a stupor, I do not know.

I felt a gentle hand on my shoulder, a familiar hand. "Frannie, it's me, Marty." It couldn't be, but when I came to my senses, there he was. I threw my arms around him and kissed him hard on the lips. He kissed me back and held me tight.

We pulled away, our arms still around each other. He looked at me with kindness I did not deserve. "I knew I would find you here," he said. I hugged him again so hard I could have hurt him. He was all flesh and bones. He gave me his handkerchief to wipe my blotchy face and blow my red runny nose.

"Come on," he said. "I think we've had enough of this."

He struggled to his feet leaning on a dark wooden cane. I wanted to help him but resisted the impulse. We took the elevator down and exited to the gardens next to the Veterans Memorial Building. He held on to my elbow all the way. He winced once, and we stopped for him to catch his breath. "I'm still getting used to this new leg," he said without self-pity. But I pitied him.

He said he was starting school again at San Francisco State. He was thinking about becoming a college history professor. I told him about my little brother Ernie and the novel I was reading. Both of us talked nonsense as if it were any other ordinary day. The German invasion of Poland made it anything but an ordinary day. Neither of us mentioned Spain.

His mustache was gone. He again looked like the preppy young man with the adorable smile I first met. Only now the indelible sadness of Spain etched itself in premature worry lines and a sag in his shoulders.

We walked a little further along the dirt path into the garden. Then I helped him sit down on a green wrought iron bench nestled between a couple of leafy poplar trees. Pink, yellow and white chrysanthemum flower beds scented the air. I sat beside him, a safe distance between us. When he was settled, he rested his hands on the curved top of the cane. The sky was now a vivid blue, the fog gone, the warming sun glittering off the dome of city hall across the street. No one else was in the garden, and only a few people walked Van Ness Avenue.

"I've got to say it, Marty," I began. "I'm sorry for…."

"Stop," he said firmly, anticipating what was coming. "I went to Spain for you, but I went for myself too. And the longer we were there the more I believed in what we were doing." He said it with the conviction of one who's earned the right. "If I had the chance I'd do it all over again."

I lowered my head. "I'm so ashamed," I said.

"We all did things we're ashamed of."

"At least I never lied to you."

Marty stretched his wooden leg and rubbed the stump, then settled back. A near-empty streetcar clanged its bell as it pulled away from the stop on Van Ness. An odd hush suffused the usually bustling street. "That Spanish nurse told me you saved my life," he said.

Thoughts of the Russian major snuck back into my mind, so I changed the subject. "You know what bothers me most is I don't like losing to those bastards. I want a rematch."

He chuckled.

"I'm serious."

"I'm sure you are."

"More children and women and old men are going to be killed," I said referring to the coming conflict. "And many young men."

"I'll do something to help when America gets in it," he said. "If it weren't for this," he tapped on his false leg with his cane, "I'd do something right now. You? You don't have to wait."

As so often happened when I talked to Marty, what must be done became evident. "Canada is going to fight with the British now. I'm going to join up." The way I blurted it out must have sounded as if I'd thought everything through already. I hadn't. But as soon as I said it I knew it was right.

"I wish I could come with you," he said. He took my hand in his and looked at me with those deep dark eyes.

I hesitated, reluctant to speak what was in my heart. But if I learned anything, I learned you had to say what you had to say while you still could. I kissed him lightly and tenderly on the lips. When he kissed me back, everything in the world finally felt right again.

"There are all kinds of love," I said when I pulled back. "I'm only starting to figure that out. What I know is I've never met anyone as good as you, or anyone I loved more."

"Please Frannie. You don't have to...."

"Don't stop me. I need to say it. I love you. When this is over and I come back, I want to marry you if you'll have me."

He ran his fingers across my cheek, then kissed me on the forehead. He smiled. "I'll never stop loving you, no matter what. But you can't come back here, at least not to stay. There will always be another war, another righteous cause, and you will always need to be there to fight it."

I wanted to argue with him, to tell him he was wrong, to tell him I loved him and would come back to him to live our lives together forever. Instead, I wrapped my arms around him and hugged him desperately.

I wished he wasn't right.

SHIPMATES

Kevin Harris

Recruit Training Center/Navy Training Center (RTC/NTC). Orlando, FL—1984

hadn't been in RTC/NTC Orlando a week yet when, lying in my bunk below Stone's at lights out, I heard jeers and blown kisses from nearly all eighty-some recruits to Clauveau. This had gone on for days until one night—with the commanding officers gone for the night—Stone, Bradley, and others, including Clauveau's own bunkmate, surrounded him as I witnessed them all at once punching, kicking, and even "flogging" him with their belts while he lay on the floor in his underwear in a fetal position sobbing and screaming. No one else besides Clauveau himself was immediately discharged from basic training in just two weeks, because his bunkmate had discovered he was gay. I had barely known and interacted with Clauveau, who was an average-looking recruit—white with a medium build—and seemed to be a really nice guy. He was also one of the recruits I had first met on the plane trip here to Orlando. However, judging from the mock high-voiced taunts wishing him, "Good night, Clauveau!" followed by whistles and smooching sounds, I had already suspected Clauveau had a secret about him that got blown or why else would the other recruits treat him like the company bitch? I already felt sorry for him and yet I barely knew him. All I felt, for the most part, was frightened—helpless.

As for me, a young black man—I had just turned nineteen—who stood all of six-feet tall but with little weight to support it, I had my own battles to fight in a barracks full of homo-hating recruits—Stone and Bradley in particular—in a mock Navy ship setting under prison-like conditions. We all referred to each other by our last names as stenciled in black ink above the left breast pocket and white ink above the right back pocket of our working blue dungaree uniforms—all of us looking like Alcatraz prison inmates except for the sailor caps the Navy officially calls "covers" and under the supervision of two commanding officers, Chief Petty Officer Fields and Petty Officer First Class Harper.

Like me, Stone and Bradley were black; however, race mattered little compared to how either tough or soft you were—just like in a prison or jail. Initially, in Stone and Bradley's eyes, both my chief nemeses, I was a faggot, too, largely because of how shy and soft-spoken I was and how timidly I smiled at them. Bradley, in particular, imitated me, using a Michael Jackson voice and the breathlessness of Marilyn Monroe, trying to break me. As difficult as it was for me to endure this form of abuse, I wasn't about to give either one of them the satisfaction that they could break me as easily as they had Clauveau, much less give them a reason to beat me down, too.

A muscular, fast-talking recruit from Cincinnati, Bradley once compared my slender thighs to his impressive biceps in front of Stone and the other recruits just to make an example of me and wondered how I had ever passed the physical for Navy recruitment. Even though I was five pounds underweight, the doctors had given me a waiver, reasoning that eight weeks of basic training would add more than the necessary pounds I needed to enhance my physique, which had encouraged me to move forward. I should have realized, however, that in the meantime I would have to endure the indignities of being an underweight recruit, including being naked among the likes of Bradley, Stone, and eighty-some other recruits when taking a shower as well as sporting Navy physical training attire or PT gear—a Navy T-shirt and gym shorts—that I would hopefully fill out after weeks of extensive physical training.

Stone, although leaner and not nearly as muscular as Bradley, still had a physique that put mine to shame, and he never passed up an opportunity to taunt me as well. "Hey, look how cute Hodges looks in his little PT uniform!" After getting his laughs, he would look me up and down and sneer. "Man, you ain't got *no* physique, do you?" And then, just as things couldn't seem to get any worse and right after our commanding officers called all recruits to stand at attention in front of our respective bunks facing each other on both the port and starboard sides of the barracks, Stone stood uncomfortably close to me—on purpose. I turned and watched his profile, his thick lips and long neck simulating a goose, his eyes half-shut with a silly grin on his face. Next thing I knew he was stroking my left shoulder.

"Quit it! What the fuck do you think you're doing!" I whispered frantically.

"Aw c'mon, Hodges, you know you like it," he replied.

I slapped his hand away.

"Quit fucking with me, Stone. I'm not playing with you."

Stone paid me no mind and then we both drew the others' attention, including recruits who stood directly facing us on the port side of the barracks while remaining at attention but bit their bottom lips to keep from laughing. My face flashed hot, and then my slaps soon became shoves and then punches. Stone stopped after that, but only because we drew dagger eyes from our commanding officers.

"What's going on over there?" said Chief Petty Officer Fields, a portly white man in a khaki dress uniform.

"Nothing, sir!" Stone and I said, almost in unison.

"Then shut up! Eyes forward! Arms at attention! IS THAT UNDERSTOOD?!"

"YES SIR!!" We both shouted in unison. And that was that.

Apparently, CPO Fields had been aware of Stone's antics, because I soon found myself with a new bunkmate and Stone wound up going through IT—intensive training—in which recruits were subjected to extra physical training—push-ups, sit-ups, and so forth—by sadistic trainers—from recruit taskmasters to officers—in a special facility with dim lighting. Of course now it took me some time to convince Bradley and other recruits close to Stone that I didn't fink on Stone to CPO Fields and Petty Officer First Class Harper.

PO1 Harper, the junior commanding officer of our company, looked like a Navy pilot judging from the shades he sported along with his Navy dress white uniform or "Cracker Jack" uniform as worn by Navy personnel during the summer. He was a thirtyish white man with black wavy hair and younger and handsomer than CPO Fields. PO1 Harper enjoyed calling us all "maggots," with a note of humor in his voice and a crooked smile, making him more endearing than intimidating. However, PO1 Harper could be just as cruel as my "shipmates" whenever I screwed up and made excuses for my mistakes, even mimicking me in a nasty namby-pamby voice. PO1 Harper only got mean with recruits who tried his patience; in this case Bradley was his most frequent target. Despite Bradley's awesome black-marbled statuesque physique, intimidating stare, and belligerence towards the likes of me who dared cross him—all of which likened him to John Amos of *Good*

Times—PO1 Harper nevertheless made a public example of him to enforce discipline, seeing Bradley as nothing more than what he really was—a bullshit artist.

On one occasion during a practice locker inspection, Bradley had ruined one of his sailor hats with what appeared to be a spot of black shoe polish. Although PO1 Harper reprimanded him, telling him his cover was no good now, Bradley tried to suppress his laughter, biting his bottom lip while remaining in attention.

"I don't see how you find this funny," Harper said silently, staring straight into Bradley's eyes. "I don't like your attitude, Bradley."

It was a wonder that PO1 Harper didn't slap that silly grin off Bradley's face, clearly leaving him with a warning—a warning Bradley didn't heed.

Then, one Saturday before a routine cadence marching, PO1 Harper rallied all recruits outside of the barracks to stand at attention in a five-abreast formation, when suddenly he screamed: "Bradley! Bradley!! What the fuck are you doing?!" Our company was facing away from the barracks when PO1 Harper reportedly ran up to Bradley in one of the back rows and tackled him into the bushes in front of the barracks. But I remained rigidly at attention—as presumably did all the other recruits—facing away from the barracks and the incident. After all, despite PO1 Harper's outburst, we had received no further orders. My guess was that PO1 Harper had caught Bradley breaking formation to pee in the bushes before he pushed him down—I know I would've reacted that way if I found an insolent recruit like Bradley doing that on my watch. At any rate, the company proceeded with marching as if nothing had happened. What else could we do? And it was because we all—Bradley and Stone included—were subject to these kinds of actions from commanding officers trying to mold us into tough U.S. Navy men that I found myself less intimidated by Bradley and, in fact, started to bond with him and the rest of my company, as it didn't seem unreasonable to believe that despite how obnoxious he acted towards me, he might be the kind of man who'd have my back—maybe even take a bullet for me in times of war—and likewise he'd want me to have his. After all, we were all forced to shave, shower, and shit together.

***

Although our commanding officers had long replaced Stone as

my bunkmate due to his constantly harassing me, which had made the two of us together counterproductive during practice inspections, Stone was still a frequent visitor to Bradley's bunk during downtime. Nevertheless, I got along better with my new bunkmate, Crawford, a short white recruit with a face like Popeye, except with two good baby-blue eyes. He was also more intelligent and easier to laugh and joke with than Stone. Stone and Bradley noticed how different, how much happier I was, too.

"Hey there, Hodges… that's a big smile on your face… so ya think you gon make it?" Stone asked.

Stone, Bradley, and another recruit named Ramon were having their own bull session at Ramon's bunk next to ours and invited Crawford and me to join them. It would be my first time officially bonding with jerks who had initially made me uncomfortable.

"So I'm curious, Hodges…." Bradley began. "You're from Washington, DC, where all the fine honeys are at and you never even had a *girlfriend*? That's so weird."

"I was never that popular," I confessed, keeping in mind that Bradley reminded me of the bullies I had encountered growing up in my neighborhood in northeast Washington, in the parochial schools in both the northeast and southeast quadrants, and even in college at Howard University—all of which I attributed to as to why I had grown disgusted with life in Washington, DC. My mother, after my father had passed away when I was fourteen, was too poor to send me away to college, and despite having been an honor student, I wasn't going anywhere on a scholarship or receiving enough in financial aid. Soon, my morale had become so low that I had decided to drop out of Howard University—following my brother Leon's footsteps, who had also dropped out of school fourteen years earlier to join the Navy Reserves, except he hadn't even finished high school.

"Maybe, because you were too *little* to get noticed by girls," Ramon interjected to everyone's amusement except mine before he slapped my shoulder. "I'm just fuckin' with you, Hodges."

Ramon was from Austin, Texas, a burly, hirsute recruit with dark wavy hair growing back nicely on his block-shaped head after a Navy crew cut.

"So, I'm guessin' you never had a girlfriend or even got laid, am I right?" Bradley asked.

I nodded, reluctantly I might add.

"Ya know, Hodges, if I was a woman right now, I'd wanna marry you, cuz you're honest," Bradley said, which took me aback. "See, dudes usually be bullshittin' about pussy they ain't never had, when all the time we know they're some lyin' motherfuckas…but not you!"

"Is that why you decided to join the Navy, Hodges? To get laid?" Crawford asked.

"Yeah, you might say that," I said.

As this pow-wow bull session continued before lights out, all of us in our underwear or as we called them "skivvies," I felt, despite the uncomfortable subject involving my sex life—or lack thereof—some degree of acceptance. What I didn't tell them, however, not even my bunkmate Crawford, was that I had been a college student at Howard University who had endured much of the same angst with women as I had had at my Catholic high school in northeast Washington and that many of the high school alumni had also become my college nemeses as well. For now, given their limited vocabulary, Bradley, Stone, and Ramon didn't strike me as guys who had ever seen the inside of a college—and—to be fair—were perhaps too young. Nevertheless, I didn't want to attract any further scrutiny regarding my virginity.

When asked if I had even seen porn flicks, I told them that the closet I'd come to seeing sex on films was when I was thirteen and my elder brother Leon used to have a sixteen millimeter projector on which he had shown highlights of blaxploitation films like *Sweet Sweetback's Baadassss Song*, *Shaft*, and *Coffey*, except the explicit sex scenes had been edited out.

"Well, you ain't seen nothin' yet until you see some real hardcore fuck flicks," Stone told me.

Just then, our recruit yeoman, one of three taskmasters besides the recruit chief petty officer and the master-at-arms, arrived with his clipboard to announce each of our next individually assigned locations following basic training here at RTC/NTC Orlando. Mine would be in Meridian, Mississippi, at Navy Technical Training Center for administrative training at a Yeoman "A" School. Much to my surprise—and chagrin—so was Bradley's.

"Wow, Hodges! How you like that?" Bradley said with enthusiasm that I didn't share. "We'll hang out and I'm gonna *throw* the pussy at you!"

Although I looked forward to Yeoman "A" School in Meridian, and, of course, interacting with female Navy personnel away from this all-male prisonlike facility, and—yes—the possibility of getting laid, I wasn't enamored of having Bradley, of all people, as a running buddy, and even less having him dictate the terms of my sexual encounters. Meanwhile, I wasn't getting much sleep—still thinking about Clauveau and the other recruits'savagery towards him—Bradley among the meanest—calling him "faggot" and whipping him mercilessly with belt straps as he lay on the floor in his skivvies crying in pain.

During the final two-mile run that all companies partook in after graduation day around the track of a vast indoor gymnasium, Bradley ran by my side the whole time "coaching" me. Every moment I felt like quitting, he kept counting out loud how many more laps we had left. This was the final test standing in the way between the rigors of boot camp and Yeoman "A" School training in Meridian.

"Okay, Hodges, three more laps!" Bradley said, amid the din of various companies of recruits running, shouting, and cussing in the acoustic-filled gymnasium, which reeked with perspiration, as I continued to chug along in excruciating pain. "If you give up now, you're a real pussy, Hodges…. C'mon! Two more laps to go…. You can do it!"

I was now torn between pushing harder after God knows how many laps and giving in to the pain and stiffness I felt all over, but I didn't want to end up walking around in the center of the track in a counter direction to the runners—like the mostly overweight recruits, including even our loud-mouthed master-at-arms—who had already given up and were forced by trainers to put themselves on display as "quitters."

"One more lap, Hodges… c'mon now…. Dig! Dig!"

With that I felt a sudden jolt of renewed energy, realizing I had just one more lap to run around the wide circumference of the track before I collapse from pain and exhaustion. Then it was over. I passed.

***

Naval Technical Training Center (NTTC)--Meridian, Mississippi

If the pilot had told me that we were now arriving in Dublin, Ireland, instead of Meridian, Mississippi, U.S.A., I probably would have believed him because of the lush green hills surrounding the Naval Technical Training Center. The Navy base itself—save for the uniformed Navy and Marine Corps personnel—reminded me of a college campus, and unlike RTC in Orlando, male and female trainees interacted on a regularly basis. The military modules were like college dormitories, and just like the barracks at RTC, they were segregated— that is, the modules were the only living quarters that didn't allow male and female Navy personnel to cohabitate, and, of course, there was a chow hall.

I finally got settled in and met my two new roommates—both of them white—Dowd and Larson. Dowd had a round face and glasses to match, and Larson was taller with steely blue eyes and a no-nonsense demeanor, as I would find out later that he had also trained in Orlando as a recruit chief petty officer in a company previous to mine.

Bradley got settled in a room adjacent to mine, which meant— much to my misfortune—he and I were neighbors. Despite how grateful I was to him for his encouragement to help me get through the rigors of boot camp, his abrasive personality still left me uneasy. Even more embarrassing, especially in the company of others, he'd call me "Junior"—despite the fact that I was two years his senior—owing to his idea of having carried me through boot camp like a protective father.

It was not uncommon for two people, however different they were- -as in the case of Bradley and me--to bond under tough circumstances as we had during basic training in Orlando—especially since Bradley and I had been company "originals." We had both witnessed other recruits either arriving from more advanced units than ours after getting set back for either disciplinary reasons or for failing to cut it in either a personnel inspection or Navy academic test, while Clauveau ended up getting harassed, physically abused, and discharged for being gay.

One recruit in particular, Nelson, who was also here in Meridian for Yeoman "A" School training, had been one of many recruits set back from another unit more advanced in its weeks of basic training into our unit. He was a meek, pale-looking white recruit with a face like a young Woody Allen, except with a wider head—a real sad sack. Bradley, Stone, and other recruits had often made fun of him, calling him ugly, and it didn't help that like other Navy recruits who wore glasses, Nelson had been issued GI glasses with thick black reinforced frames—"birth control glasses." Nelson's problems, however, ran deeper, owing largely to his lack of confidence, not to mention his rejection from a previous, more advanced company than ours. Bradley and Stone had sometimes compared me to Nelson whenever I had felt inadequate and ready to give up—but only to rile me enough to push harder. At least Nelson had made it this far and didn't have to worry about Stone anymore, who had been assigned to remain in Orlando to train as a fireman. Also, unlike myself, Nelson didn't have Bradley as a module neighbor.

On my first day at NTTC Meridian, as I was unpacking my government-issued sea bag of all my Navy gear, Dowd, who was alone with me in the room, approached me, asking if I was a "regular guy"—that is, someone who preferred reading to listening to loud rap music he'd heard from the other residents (most of them black) who played cassettes on "boomboxes" in the module lounge area surrounded by three bedrooms, each one occupied by three roommates. Dowd was relieved when I told him that I usually listened to music on a Walkman, watching me curiously the whole time when I spoke.

"You don't *sound* black," he said.

Somewhat taken aback but slightly amused, I replied, "Okayyy... do I *look* black?"

"Yeah, um, no... I mean, you don't sound like the ones I know.... Like the guys I know here."

It seemed just looking at Dowd's round, bespectacled face that I could tell he hadn't been around black people much--if at all--prior to here.

"Where are you from, Dowd?"

"Boston," he said.

"I'm from Washington, DC," I said. "Did you do basic training in Orlando, too?"

"No, Great Lakes."

"I see."

"The guy here before you, he was black, too, and just like the others who listen to that loud music and hung out with them. When he left I thought 'good riddance!'"

"Hmmm," I said, feigning amusement.

Dowd referred to the same music I had heard last in DC—mostly when I had last attended Howard University when I was in the College of Fine Arts department—from music groups like Musical Youth and Mtume—and all across campus I had mostly heard Prince, The Time, and Michael Jackson. In the inner city, including my own neighborhood in northeast Washington, it was Chuck Brown and the Soul Searchers and Doug E. Fresh—the same music even my brother, who was ten years my senior, listened to in his bedroom.

Bradley—no surprise—blended in nicely with many of the module residents, including his roommate Payne, a shaven-headed black man with a loud, ringing, high-pitched voice that reverberated throughout the module like a fire alarm. He could be overhead during a conversation in the lounge in the middle of disagreeing and often heard saying: "I DOUBT IT!!" Dowd, who usually preferred to stay alone lying on his back in his top bunk above his bunkmate's with either a heavy mystery novel or political nonfiction (he was a Republican), hated Payne most of all not only because he was loud, but also—as he even told him—incomprehesible. When I asked Dowd why he chose to remain in his room and not watch TV in the lounge with the rest of us, he told me candidly—emphatically, I might add: "Let me get something straight: I have absolutely no communication with these people!"

I likened Dowd to disgraced former president Richard M. Nixon and was reminded of a joke Richard Pryor had made about Nixon after the Watergate scandal—about how Nixon wouldn't last ten minutes in jail if he were locked up in the same cell with black inmates. But instead of confronting Dowd on what he had meant by his "these people" remark, I let it go. Also, as much as I hated to admit it, despite having the same skin color I felt just as alienated by "these people" as he did, but largely because I was comparatively unhip and still a virgin. Dowd was white, unhip, and, apparently even more alone.

Meanwhile, Bradley, myself, Nelson, and other trainees, many of whom I remembered as former RTC/NTC Orlando recruits in my company, were in the typing class—that is, a classroom for yeoman trainees who needed to get up to a minimum of 20 words per minute before commencing Yeoman "A" School courses. During those first few days Bradley and I partook in cadence marching in the same company among five others consisting of yeoman and aviation trainees, all of us marching five abreast in working blue dungaree uniforms with one trainee in the front row of each company as the flagbearer. When classes ended late in the afternoon, we'd all march back to our respective modules, after which I usually watched television in the lounge with Dowd. When the evening arrived somebody would rent a movie— sometimes an X-rated one—and the lounge would suddenly become crowded with Bradley, Payne, our enormous module section leader Mason, and guests from other modules, at which time Dowd would retreat back to his room presumably to read and avoid the crowd. I, on the other hand, remained—more out of curiosity than anything else to check out hardcore porn flicks or the like—including *Debbie Does Dallas, Hot Lips*, and so on--ignoring the thin plot and often silly dialogue, if any.

On one such evening, Bradley had brought along Charleston, another former Navy recruit from boot camp and now Bradley's pal here in Meridian. Other recruits had nicknamed Charleston "Charlie Brown" because in profile he resembled the *Peanuts* comic strip character. Although generally friendlier and more easy-going than Bradley, Charleston, a big, tall, white guy, was also annoying, largely because he laughed at practically everything Bradley said and did, usually at my expense. Bradley, Charleston, and the others delighted in my reactions and comments over watching porn flicks featuring buxom starlets, some of whom were lesbians tongue-kissing one another while others participated in a threesome, usually consisting of a man and two women.

"Well, Junior, how do you like these flicks?" Bradley asked me.

"Stop calling me Junior," I protested.

"Ah, ah! Don't talk back to your father now," said Charleston wagging his finger.

"So what are you my mom now?" I said snidely, to which Charleston took his folded cover and playfully slapped me over the head with it.

Other guests besides Charleston included nutty aviation trainees—usually friends of the other mod residents—who'd drop in from time to time to check out the "fuck flicks." Although I didn't particularly like these guys, sitting here drinking beer and chilling out on porn flicks with them made me less uncomfortable.

"I promise, you, Hodges... We gonna hook you up with pussy like that, you'll see!" Bradley said, who was seated next to me on the opposite side of Charleston.

"Fine, fine..." I said, waving him off, in part because I wanted to watch the flicks in peace, and in part because I didn't want him hinting I was a virgin, even though it was probably no secret to anyone now.

***

Finally, I got my typing speed up fast enough to leave the typing class and begin official Yeoman "A" School training. The black hardbound binder I carried to school with me contained a yeoman study and reference guide for open-book use in class. The guide was so de-tailed, however, that more often than not I rushed through instructions without thoroughly reading them and ended up have to redo a les-son topic administered by my civilian instructor Mr. Cobbs, a retired white-haired Marine colonel with a raspy Mississippi drawl, reading glass, and a pot belly. Right now, I struggled with how to properly write and format a Navy correspondence draft on letterhead stationary. Mr. Cobbs called me up to his desk.

"Hodges, have yew ever considered goin' to night school?" he asked me.

"No, sir."

"Welp, yer goin' now!" he said, much to my dismay.

Meanwhile, I continued to struggle with the stress of what I had witnessed months ago back at RTC/NTC Orlando, and still losing sleep when remembering Clauveau crying out in pain each time Brad-ley, Stone, or another recruit had brought his strap down upon him while he lay pathetically on the barracks floor in his skivvies trying to shield himself. Also, I found myself nodding off in class sometimes when trying to read.

Dowd's old roommate, Larson, had completed his training and was shipping off to his permanent assignment elsewhere, making room for his replacement, who made his first appearance overnight as a large, statuesque silhouette just two hours or so before it was time to get up for school, whispering to me, "What's happening, shipmate?" His last name was Tyson, and in the daylight he was a muscular, heavy-set black man—though not as obese as our mod section leader Mason and not quite as rock-solid as Bradley—as he sat on Larson's old bunk below Dowd's—his skivvies revealing massive biceps and thighs. The anatomy term to best describe Tyson—as he described himself—was a "mesomorph." He told me that he had read anatomy textbooks—and, begrudgingly, I might add—I accepted his description of me as an "ec-tomorph."

"I've never met anyone who also understood anatomy terms!" Ty-son told me, showing the widest, toothiest smile I had seen worn on any shipmate.

"I took anatomy drawing at Howard University."

"Oh, so you already attended college?"

"No shit, Hodges?" asked Dowd, overhearing our discussion. He sat up in his bunk. "I should have guessed."

"That's Dowd," I informed Tyson, motioning to Dowd with my head.

"Nice to meet you, man," Tyson said, rising up from the bottom bunk to shake Dowd's hand. Dowd rubbed the sleep out of his eyes before he put on his glasses to get a better look at whose hand he had just shaken.

"All right, I know Navy regulations have us calling each other by our last names and shit," Tyson began. "But what say in this room we call each other by our first names. I'm Cecil."

"Kyle," I said.

We turned to Dowd. "I'm sorry, no offense, but I'm fine with 'Dowd,'" he said, holding up both hands.

"Okay, man, have it your way," Tyson said, shrugging, before turning back to me. "I like you already, Kyle."

"Likewise," I said, and meant it.

Tyson, or rather Cecil, and I became instant friends, the two of us already marching side by side among our company in five-abreast formation to school. Cecil was also attending Yeoman "A" School, but in a class separate from mine and was already an exceptional typist. We'd have lunch together in the chow hall, normally just the two of us, and then after school he'd even join Dowd and me sometimes to relax in the lounge of our module, even sticking by my side to watch porn flicks when it got even more crowded. He also seemed to get along with Bradley, Charleston, and the rest of the crew doing his own share of bullshitting and cussing as well. Bradley had finally gotten his typing speed up for official yeoman training as well and—thankfully—was in a different classroom, too.

Nelson had finally advanced from the typing class, and now we shared the same class in which all yeoman trainees must not only pass each lesson topic successfully without exceeding two attempts, but also get their typing speed up to a minimum of 25 words per minute to be "A" qualified. Although I was still struggling with a series of Navy correspondence letters using letterhead stationary under the fictitious Navy vessel "USS John A. Bole," I did meet, even exceed, the minimum typing speed to be "A" qualified. Nelson, on the other hand, struggled all around, showing no sign of improvement whatsoever—and one day I found him standing at parade rest in front of wall with a "X" painted on it outside in the hallway through the classroom door window, a worried expression on his meek, bespectacled face. It wouldn't be long before I knew exactly what kind of trouble Nelson was in because in just a few days I was next in line.

Mr. Cobbs called me up to his desk after dismissal to fill out out a form that included the following headings in bold letters: **How Often Do You Study?** to which I wrote down: At least twice a week. It was a lie. I had mistakenly assumed that because the classroom sessions were open-book I didn't need to. The other heading read: **Reason For Failure?** Now I was scared.

"Well it *should* frighten you, Hodges. You're going to have to face the review board tomorrow. So if I were yew, I'd do some serious soul searchin'," said Mr. Cobbs.

"*Review* board?" I repeated, choking. "You mean I'm about to be expelled?"

"That's up to the board... it's outta mah hands now! You failed five topics under Navy correspondence, which put you behind."

"Please, Mr. Cobbs, sir... I-I didn't realize... I thought it was all open-book."

"Tell that to the board, Hodges. In the meantime go on back to your mod and sleep it off."

And that was that.

I arrived back to my mod shaken by what had just happened and not saying a word to anyone; however, it became apparent to my roommates Cecil and Dowd, along with Payne, whom Cecil had invited into our the room, that something was wrong because of my reticence instead of my interaction over the usual bullshit. Dowd, who had been attending aviation night classes himself, and who had spent most his time away from the others either reading or brooding about his own future, zeroed in on my dilemma.

"If you're in trouble because of school, Hodges, it can't be as bad as all that... Look, I've been here a long time... long before you and Tyson arrived here, wondering why they haven't kicked me out already."

I sat at the foot of my bed, downcast. Cecil placed his hand on my shoulder, "Is that what's got you down, man? You're behind in your yeoman training courses?"

"Worse...." I muttered.

"What happened, Kyle?" Cecil asked.

Keeping my head down I told them.

"Oh, shit! Hodges...." said Payne.

"How did you get so far behind, Kyle? Haven't you been studying?"

Cecil asked.

I shook my head. "I've only been using my study guide in class when looking up the answers."

"Oh, no *wonder*, Kyle!" Cecil exclaimed, almost laughing. "Look, man, I'm sure it won't be as bad as all that... just tell the board what happened, that's all."

"Yo, what's goin' on in there?" shouted Bradley from outside in the lounge, just as Payne had already left the room, closing the door after him and filling Bradley in before I got a chance to tell Payne not to. Next, I overheard Bradley's reaction.

"Aw no, what kind of trouble did Hodges get himself into now?" he said.

Nobody prevented Bradley from entering, preferring instead to head outside to the lounge. Cecil, however, patted my shoulder before doing so, leaving me alone to my own devices.

Shirtless and wearing beige swim trucks—the same one issued to all Navy recruits—Bradley stood before me with a hard expression that matched the muscles of his chest, arms, legs, and so on, his coal-dark skin glistening with sweat from the heat of the afternoon sun. I remained seated at the foot of my bed, bracing myself for his verbal assaults, my study guide on my lap.

"So, you're in trouble with the review board, too, huh? Ha! Just like that loser Nelson. Well, ain't that some shit! All the time I thought you wanted to be a yeoman."

I said nothing, trying instead to ignore him by looking down on a page of my study guide as if I were alone.

"You really had everybody fooled, Hodges... especially me. I thought you'd finally loosened up, were becoming more like one of the boys instead of the punk you was in boot camp. I took you under my wing, helped get your li'l skinny ass in shape, so you could make it here. And now I find you don't have the common sense to do your *homework*?"

I knew he was mocking me, but nevertheless I lifted my head raising my eyes to meet his.

"Are you done now, Bradley? I'm trying to study," I said, feeling the anger brewing inside me.

"Hell no I ain't done! You're a real disappointment, Junior. I thought I raised you better than that... but you're every bit a loser as Nelson. Dumb-assed motherfucker!"

Now I found myself trembling, as if I had Parkinson's disease, fumbling to turn the page of my study guide, while Bradley continued his diatribe. He even went so far as to slam my binder shut each time I tried to turn the page until I exploded into a blind and violent rage that sent him rushing out of the room, yelling, "He's crazy!! Motherfucker's gone berserk!!" Cecil, Dowd, and Payne all rushed back into the room to check on me.

"What the fuck just happened? What did he *say* to you?" Cecil demanded.

"I OUGHTA KILL THAT MOTHERFUCKIN' SONABITCH!!" I heard myself screaming, as both Cecil and Payne took and held me by each arm to restrain me before I finally simmered down. Just then Mason stormed into the room from his own, looking huge in his skivvies and yelled "AY!! What's all the hollering about? Has this mod gone crazy? You know we can't have this shit!! You want the petty officers to come up in here? Besides, I'm trying to sleep!!"

"It's awright, Mason, chill! We got this!" Payne said.

Finally, I was quiet and sat back down on the foot of the bed. Cecil and Payne sat on either side of me. Dowd remained standing, a forlorn expression on his face, before he retreated to his own bunk.

"If it would make you feel any better, Hodges, I once had to face the ol' chief muhself," Payne said. "All he's gon do is review your work and then ask you some questions about whether or not you really want to be a yeoman."

Cecil patted my knee and watched me with more tenderness than normal, before he smiled. "Don't listen to Bradley's bullshit anymore.... He's not worth it. His kind will never get far. Trust me when I say that. You'll be a'ight."

I nodded, but I was still scared, uncertain.

Cecil and Payne left me alone with Dowd, and I could hear voices outside in the lounge after the door closed, including Bradley's asking how I was. I even heard Cecil saying, "Leave him alone, Bradley, don't go in there," to which Bradley replied, "Aw motherfucker, you don't even know him like that! Get outta my way!"

The door cracked open slightly before I saw Bradley's head sticking tentatively inside, before he invited himself in. I just sat quietly looking at Dowd who was lying on his back in the top bunk, shrugging.

"I just wanna talk to you, Hodges... we're boys! You and me, remember?" Bradley said, and then looked up at Dowd. "Yo! Do you mind leavin' the room, I wanna talk to my boy!"

Dowd looked at me, but I said nothing. He then hopped off his bunk and headed out the door presumably to join the others in the lounge to watch TV.

"I have nothing to say to you, Bradley," I said.

"It's cool. Look here. I didn't think you was gonna go off like that over a little ball-breakin'. Fuck, can't you take a little joke?"

"It didn't sound that way to me. And you crossed the line," I said.

"Aw, c'mon, Hodges, how you expect to make it in the Navy if you're so thin-skinned? You need to toughen up. You just can't lose your temper like a little kid."

I remained silent.

"But make me understand somethin', Hodges. If you been through college, how come you can't handle yeoman training?"

Previously, I had eventually told Beasley upon arriving here in Meridian that I had attended Howard University, but what I hadn't told him until now was that I had also been an art major.

"*Art?*" Bradley said loudly. "Oh, so that means it must have been a while since you took reading courses an' shit, huh?"

"Yeah, something like that," I said, leaving out that I had been an honor student in high school as well, because I didn't want him to use that information against me.

"I swear, Hodges, you and Nelson are just about exactly alike…. You both lack confidence, you're both weak, and quite frankly, you're both stupid!"—and then he burst out laughing. "I'm just fuckin' wid you, Hodges, you're still my boy!"

And then he was gone.

Cecil, who had been at NTTC Meridian in just two weeks, had not only gotten well ahead of me in Yeoman "A" School, but had also exceeded the course curriculum, which made me a tad jealous. Thus, he had plenty of time to go out to the local Enlisted Men's Club and dance with many Navy female personnel, looking dapper in his dress white crackerjack uniform—the same one he had passed a recent Navy personnel inspection in with an "outstanding" rating—and rarely got turned down for slow dancing with an attractive woman whenever a slow jam like "Purple Rain" came up. During a fast jam amid the flashing lights, Cecil practically brought down the entire EM Club, dancing tip-toed and buckling his legs rhythmically to the music while gliding across the dance floor like a spinning top to tunes like "Erotic City."

For a slightly overweight, yet muscular guy, Cecil was incredibly light on his feet and downright electrifying on the dance floor.

Not long after my hearing with the review board, Cecil offered to help me study most evenings after school—that is, the evenings I wasn't scheduled for night school or when Dowd was attending night school himself, leaving the two of us with the room to ourselves. I also endeavored to not only catch up in class, but also to sail through the course curriculum as quickly as Cecil.

During our study sessions, Cecil told me that prior to the Navy he had been studying to become a computer programmer and had taken classes in the field in Chicago, where he was from. He would sometimes quiz me, holding my study guide while I recited answers or tried to. Earlier sessions with Cecil were fun, but occasionally rigorous, because Cecil could switch from being his normal jovial self to the same no-nonsense mentality of a recruit chief petty officer. During breaks, we'd laugh and joke about others here in Meridian, even our roommate Dowd and his stiffness around the other mod residents. We'd also swap boot camp tales—that is, his stories in Great Lakes and mine in Orlando. Sitting together on the edge of my bed, the two of us in our PT uniforms, I even told him about how PO1 Harper had once pushed Bradley in the bushes after he caught him urinating in them (at least, that was my impression) and how gradually I had bonded with Bradley and others to gain their respect.

"Yeah, but don't you see how he's been treating you lately? How he uses how he helped you get through boot camp just to fuck over you?" Cecil said frankly. "Have you forgotten already the way he cut you down and made you lose your cool? You're not in boot camp anymore."

I paused. Cecil was right, of course.

"It's none of my business, really, but I don't think you should hang with him anymore—at least not outside of this mod," Cecil said. "I've known dudes like him all my life—they have that streetlike mentality to use nice guys like you to their advantage."

Although what Cecil was telling me resonated, I didn't want to discuss it anymore. Instead, I wanted to resume studying… quietly. I took the black hardbound binder containing my yeoman reference guide and went over tomorrow's lesson topics. Cecil, who sat uncomfortably close me, remained quiet, as I could hear him breathing, as if trying to make up his mind what to say next. Then, subtly, as once before when I hadn't thought to say anything, he put his hand on my back, patting it, and then gently began rubbing it making swirling motions. Immediately, I saw flashbacks of Stone during my early weeks in boot camp in Orlando standing too close to me and patting my shoulder, before making the same swirling motions just to fuck with me, saying, *C'mon, Hodges, you know you like it!* before I had slapped his hand away angrily. Now I found myself up on my feet, staring down at a stunned Cecil.

"Just what the hell are you doing?" I said.

"Oh, man… Kyle, I'm sorry, I thought you were sad about what I said, so I was comforting you…"

"It felt like more than that to me!" I said, trembling a little, more out of embarrassment than anger.

Cecil then let air out of his nostrils, and then stood up facing me. "Okay, man, first of all, I'm sorry for getting the wrong idea."

"Oh *man*, you're *gay*?"

"Just call me a bisexual brother," Cecil said, a subtle crooked smile reaching his face.

"And you think I'm gay, too?"

"Well…"

"Well, I'm *not*! Okay? So let's make that clear!" I finally said.

"I'm sorry, Kyle."

I then put my hand over my forehead. "How could that be? I see you dancing all the time and flirting with women. You even talk about pussy as much as anybody else!"

"And you don't, Kyle," Cecil said. "You're nothing like those other jerks, that's what I find special about you."

"Well, I'm sorry to disappoint you, but I'm not gay… okay? I love women."

"Okay, okay, Kyle. Damn. Stop getting so defensive."

I began pacing back and forth in front of him.

"Tell me. Who else knows you're bisexual?"

"Nobody. Just you… at least here."

"What do you mean?"

"Trust me. I know the military frowns upon gays, but you'd be surprised how many gays are already serving. And it's not a bad thing, Kyle."

"Okay, you're telling me you knew other gay recruits at Great Lakes, too?"

"Sure, haven't you run into any in Orlando?"

"Well, there was someone named Clauveau who was in our company. He was just one of the recruits I had first met on the plane trip to Orlando. Bradley and other recruits harassed him and later gave him a beat down... first punching, then kicking him, and then whipping him with their belt straps while he was still in his underpants because they found out he was gay, too."

"Jesus," Cecil said. "So what happened to him?"

"You mean besides getting a beat down? He got discharged, that's what happened."

Cecil shook his head. "So is that why I see you sometimes tossing and turning in your sleep? You saw it go down, didn't you?"

I paused, then I nodded. "And it's been tearing me up inside. I barely even *knew* Clauveau, but I still felt like a coward watching Bradley and the others beat him like that. It was horrible."

"What could you have done, Kyle? It wasn't your fault. And, don't worry, I'm not afraid of Bradley, but I don't want to get discharged, either. I joined the Navy for the same reasons as anyone else, and I don't want any trouble. I can trust you to keep this between us, right?" "Yeah, man..." I said. "Because you know I don't want any trouble, either."

Just then, Dowd returned. "Hey fellas."

"What's up, Dowd?" Cecil said, before heading back to his bottom bunk below Dowd's and talking his usual bullshit. He even told him how I was progressing in my studies, to which I feigned a smile before I got ready for bed.

Cecil, Dowd, and I still met occasionally for dinner at the chow hall; however, it wasn't the same as before, as Dowd sensed some tension between Cecil and me, noticing my reticence and Cecil limiting his conversation to just him. One night, with Cecil out of the room, Dowd finally asked me if it had something to do with why we were no longer studying together. I told him, "I just told Cecil that I didn't need his help anymore, that's all, and that I'm doing better in school now."

"Oh, well then he must be taking it pretty hard," Dowd said.

I sighed, preferring that Dowd drop the subject entirely. I was also nervous about Bradley and the others somehow finding out about Cecil, too, remembering what Bradley and the other recruits back then had done to Clauveau at RTC Orlando—and worried now that Bradley and his new pals here in Meridian might even gang up on me, too, for associating with Cecil.

The following weekend, Bradley, Charleston, and others including fellow mod residents all knocked on my door one evening, inviting Cecil and me to a night on the town. Even though Dowd was in the room, too, he was not invited. Cecil, however, declined the invitation and hinted that I should, too; however, acting out of sheer boredom, especially with the lingering tension between Cecil and me, I decided to go along.

We all wore our various dress white uniforms as we all first went out to see a movie—*The Terminator*—followed by dinner afterwards and drinks at the bar of a local tavern. I was actually enjoying everyone's company—even Bradley's, who seemed friendlier than normal and less disparaging towards me in the others' presence, including his sidekick's Charleston. As the night progressed, however, and the more we drank, I noticed Bradley whispering to Charleston, before they in turn whispered to the others, including two others sailors I didn't know who had ridden along with us, before all of them surrounded my bar stool.

"We got a surprise for you, Hodges," said Bradley.

I forced a smile, but inside I felt very uneasy. "Okay... what's up?"

"We hired a hooker!" said Charleston. "She agreed to get you laid. After tonight you won't be a virgin anymore!"

"*What!*" I yelled. "Are you crazy?"

"No we're normal! You're the one who's either crazy or *gay* if you turn down this opportunity!" Bradley said, making Charleston and the others laugh.

"C'mon, Hodges, think of it as a *celebration!*" said Payne. "You got past the review board, didn't you?"

"And you made it through boot camp before that, with my help and encouragment!" Bradley added.

"Look, fellas, maybe this isn't right," said Mason. "If Hodges isn't ready then maybe we shouldn't push him."

"Oh, sure.... He'd rather spend it like a pussy with Twinkle Toes Tyson and dorky Dowd!" Bradley said. "How long you gonna wait, Hodges? You wanna go home the same punk you were before you enlisted? I thought you wanted to get laid!"

"Yeah, but not like *that!*" I said.

"Aw don't worry, Hodges, if it's money you're worried about, you're covered. We already paid her, so, don't let us down!" Bradley said, stabbing his finger into my chest with his last four words.

"*What?*" I replied.

"Aw leave him alone, man," said one of the sailors I didn't know, a seemingly older

black man named Colt. "He scared! Can't you see that? He ain't no man. He's a fucking *pussy!*"

That was it. I couldn't take it anymore—the uneasiness I felt around Cecil, the peer-pressure I was enduring now—so I caved.

"Fuck it! I'm NOT a pussy! Where is she?"

Inside a Howard Johnson's motel suite just a few miles away from the NTTC Meridian base, as I lay on my back in bed a nervous stiff while already stripped down to my skivvy shorts, a prostitute—an older woman with dirty blond hair appearing to be perhaps in her midthirties, her face so caked with make-up and eyeliner that it was hard to tell her real age, and bushy false eyelashes that hung like canopies over large blue eyes with crow's feet—sat on top of me. I could only imagine now how I must have looked to her, staring up at her.

"Relax, hon. Ah'm not gonna hurt yew…" she said softly in a heavy Missisippi drawl. "This *is* what ya'll want, ain't it?"

"Y-yes!" I stammered, hearing my own voice crack.

"Your buddies told me *all* about yew…including how shah yew are."

Not long after my arrival to Meridian, I had heard rumors about this particular Howard Johnson's inn. Until now, the last time I had been to a Howard Johnson's was three years before to dine at a rest stop while returning from a family summer vacation at Busch Gardens. And now here I lay in bed in the establishment's suite watching a naked blonde on top of me kneading my chest with her palms as if she were rolling dough with a rolling pin. I watched her face and her droopy breasts—a departure from the buxom startlets I had seen on rented porn flicks. But it didn't matter… not really. It felt nice, really nice….

Next, she worked her way down to my skivvy shorts and proceeded to pull them down, leaving me feeling self-conscious, but like the pro that she was, she began stroking my cock until it was good and hard before she stuck it inside her mouth and began sucking it up and down, slurping it like a melting popsicle. She then placed it inside her, before stradling over the top of me, which felt incredible, so much so that I couldn't hold the pleasure any longer. She then lapped up my semen.

Then it was over. I was a virgin no longer.

I was so happy I wanted her to stay with me overnight and have breakfast with me in the morning, but instead, she decided to get dressed back into her leopard-skinned deep V-neck blouse that showed off her cleavage, black leather mini skirt and leopard-designed pumps matching her blouse. "That would cost yew an extra fifty along with the hundred yew still owe me now, hon."

My face flashed hot. "Beg your pardon?"

"Yew heard me, cough it up!" she said, extending out her palm.

"Wait a minute. I thought it was already covered. Didn't the fellas pay you already?"

"Are yew kiddin' me? Is that what they told yew?" she replied, giving me an incredulous look, as I now felt even more exposed than when she had pulled down my underpants.

I spent the rest of the night alone in the motel suite and ate breakfast the following morning alone as well. Although I should have been thrilled that I had finally lost my virginity, I couldn't shake the sting of what Bradley, Charleston, and the others had pulled on me, leaving me alone to pay that prostitute out of my own pocket, as I dined alone at my table on pancakes and link sausages, which despite how much I relished it seemed to taste like rubber and felt like lead in my stomach. Worse, I blamed myself for being gullible enough to believe that Bradley—of all people—would pay my way for anything. I didn't want to go back to base right away to face Cecil, or anyone else at this point.

The following night, and after too much to drink, I was at the EM Club where I spotted Bradley and Charleston among others I didn't recognize or care about sitting at a table. Angry while intoxicated I went over to Bradley's table, his back towards me as I approached. I tapped him lightly on his shoulder before he turned around and looked up.

"Yo, Hodges! Muh man! How'd it go? You got laid, right?"

"Yeah, I got laid…"

Everyone at the table shouted, congratulating me, including those sailors I didn't know. But I wasn't going to sit with them.

"You suckered me! You made me pay about a third of my paycheck to that whore! I told you I didn't want it like that, motherfucker!"

Charleston howled out loud laughing, slapping Bradley's shoulder, while the others laughed, some of them holding their mouths.

"What does it matter, Hodges? The point is you ain't a virgin no mo'! You're a man now."

"I was a man at first! And you are a fuckin' liar!! You're also a bully, a gay-basher, an instigator, and, above all, a user. *That's* why you helped me through boot camp."

"Gay-basher? What the fuck you talkin' about?" Bradley frowned.

"Don't tell me you don't remember what you and the others did to Clauveau!"

"Clauveau? That faggot motherfucker back at boot camp months ago? Why, what do you care?"

"He may have been gay, but you didn't have to beat him like that! You gay-bashing motherfucker!"

More howls arose. Bradley, however, remained calm.

"Go home, Hodges…You're drunk and I don't wanna hurt you, see? Go back to the mod an sleep it off and we're talk about it tomorrow."

"I wanna talk about it NOW!! And you still owe me money, asshole!!"

After more instigating reactions from his table, Bradley rose up slowly and gave me a stare, but I didn't back down… instead I stared back. I didn't care what happened next.

"Congratulations, Hodges. Not only did you finally get laid, you also got real heart now. You've changed a lot. I'm proud of you, Junior. Now go home."

"Fuck you!!" I shouted right to his face.

I found myself tasting the floor, my mouth full of blood seeping from my botton lip. Two sailors not from Bradley's table lifted me back up to my feet, just as another fight had broken out and Bradley was in it—with Cecil. The modestly crowded EM Club seemed suddenly packed with spectators watching Cecil and Bradley trading blows in a heavyweight slug fest like the ones I had watched between Muhammad Ali and Joe Frazier. It seemed to be even until Cecil, with all his weight, did a graceful spinning back kick, catching the right side of Bradley's face and sending him sailing clear over the table where he, Charleston, and their buddies had been sitting.

Bradley, the whole time, in fact, had been struggling with his own yeoman courses—even worse than I had—which explained why he had ridden me so hard: to disguise his own shortcomings—a bullshit artist to the very end. He was subsequently transferred out to serve aboard ship somewhere—but as a boatswain's mate—although I suspected it had more to do with other problems, such as hassling me. Sadly, Nelson had been transferred out as well—even before I had faced the review board myself. I, however, remained and not only caught up but also exceeded expectations, thanks initially to Cecil, and was eligible for on-the-job training. Best of all, I was finally able to sleep better, especially with Bradley gone, feeling less guilty about Clauveau now that I had finally confronted Bradley on the issue. My conscience was clear—at least for now.

Finally, I received orders to return home to a Navy Reserves unit in Washington, DC for weekend duty once every month, while I re-enrolled for college—except now I would be going to the University of the District of Columbia. I didn't see my bunkmates—my friends—Cecil and Dowd again.

In 1993, just months after President Bill Clinton had been elected and attempted to overturn a ban against gays and lesbians from serving in the U.S. military, I thought about Cecil and Dowd and remembered one of the last times I had entered our module room when I had caught them both in skivvies, cuddling on Cecil's bunk. Dowd had jumped up, protesting, "Don't you *knock?*" After getting over my initial shock, I had laughed nervously and replied. "Relax…I won't tell." And I had also learned that unlike Bradley, these two were *true* shipmates—and the ones I'd rather have my back in time of war.

And it was true—I had told nobody about my bunkmates while I was in Meridian. Cecil had told me later that Dowd's first name was "Sherman."

BABA YAGA, THE INTERSEX WITCH

Kathleen Murphey

I am Baba Yaga, and no one knows what to do with me. I am a bundle of contradictions—associated with winter and spring, death and life, light and dark, male and female, the wild and the domestic, age and youth, human and animal, sky and earth. Mice, crows, and foxes are my pets. I am scavenger and hunter. I am prey and predator. I scurry, I fly, and I run. I am meek and stealthy. All this and more, my pets reflect. They call me a witch because they don't understand me. Their rigid and intolerant Christian blinders don't give them the imagination to appreciate me. They would burn me if they knew. When I was young, I was magnificent: the ultimate Janus god, not future and past, but both male and female—with breasts and scrotum.

I remember one Spring Equinox in particular. It is thousands of years now in the past. But the people had painted themselves in a variety of ways. Some had painted themselves for the grains and fruits and vegetables that they hoped with come with the harvest. Others had painted themselves for the game they hoped to catch or the kids and lambs they hoped the goats and sheep would birth. The children painted themselves or were painted as mice and crows and foxes. My priestess, their consorts, and I would bless the grains and seeds that would be planted in the following days. As dark fell, the bonfires were lit. The people had been drinking wine and hard cider as they decorated themselves and prepared the bonfires. The feast would begin after the ceremony. The drums started beating. I was painted—my female breasts in a bright red color and my scrotum in bold blue. Snakes were painted coiling up my legs. Mice were painted on my arms, and I wore a black crow mask. The chanting began.

"Great One! Great One! Baba Yaga! Baba Yaga! Mysterious Baba Yaga Bring Us Spring and Harvest and Plenty! Great One! Great One!"

The priestess fussed and escorted me naked from my house. People had thrown fresh leaves on the path all the way from my little house to the village center. The platform was there. The three consorts were kneeling, waiting for the priestesses. I took my position in the center. The Great Mother and her consort, the Great Father, approached me and gave me wine and honey and fresh water. Next, the Grand Mother and Grand Father came forward with dried fruits and vegetables and nuts. Lastly, the Mother and Father brought me an egg, a piece of deer liver, and the heart of a chicken. I consumed all these things in the ritual fashion with the important blessings. Then, I turned to the grains and seeds and blessed them and asked them to grow for me and for my grateful and respectful people. We sang and danced, and I left the platform to bless the goats and sheep and chickens and our most able hunters, foragers, and farmers—in short all my people. The drums continued, and the priestess and their consorts enacted rites of spring while people around them danced and sang to the drums beating. It was a beautiful night, and we were so happy. It was a simpler and more peaceful kind of life. Our gods were many—the spirits in the streams and rivers, in the trees, in the very mountains themselves. We were bound to the earth and our cousins—the creatures all around us. We killed creatures but always with respect and thanks. And then it all began to change.

The followers of Jesus of Nazareth said he was the One True God. His trinity was the Father, Son, and Holy Ghost (only males) instead of the Mother, the Crone, and the Maiden and their consorts. Whatever policies of love and forgiveness, Jesus had taught, his followers insisted that they were only attainable through rigid intolerance of anything other. God, the Father, was a rigid sky god, placed in Heaven, ruthless, vengeful, and unforgiving. His son becomes Christ through his grue- some death by cruxfixion. Suffering and penance the only offerings Christian followers could give to attain love and forgiveness, not on earth but, in Heaven. So strange and unnatural. No feminine element or elements in Holy Trinity, no balance. Jesus' own mother must be a virgin—because sex has firmly been associated with sin and shame since Adam and Eve. So sad. Such a strange way to live. Women sub- jugated to men—inferior in the eyes of the Church and inferior in the Christian faith. Such a violent faith—how many killed in Christ's name? How many powerful men did violence to others cloaked under the (literal and figurative) veils of the Church?

But I digress. Doesn't it make sense now—that I fly through the air with both a womb and a phallus? Theoretically, I have both with my mortar and pestle. It is why I am associated with contradictory things—I am not one, but all.

My carriage, the mortar and pestle, left a mark behind. More specifically, the pestle left a trailing mark behind—as the phallus always leaves a trail or contamination and wreckage in its wake, at least in the patriarchal order. So, in addition, to the mortar and pestle, they associated me with a broom—for the Christians, the witches' means of transport, and with this broom, I swept away the marks of the pestle's passage.

My house is as contradictory as myself—a house on chicken legs. The house a symbol of a settled existence—usually a house in a village or community—and yet my house is not like others. It has legs and moves, and it is located in the woods, alone by itself. Where regular humans live in stationary houses in villages for mutual protection and security, my little house moves as it or I will and finds protection in isolation in the wilds of the woods—so un-Christian and suspicious in their self-righteous eyes.

Oh, how they have perverted my stories—Christianized them beyond recognition, so their original meanings and lessons are lost. Take for example the story of the boy who comes to become a man where my priestesses showed him the passage to the underworld and told him how to position himself to make the crossing. He was too frightened and wouldn't take the position. But the story gets twisted, and the priestesses become my daughters doing my evil bidding, and the boy tricks them and cooks them in the oven and then, to my fury, escapes home a hero instead of a coward or villain.

But, consider how the story might be told alternately. Like so many of the essential elements, fire has the powers of both life and death. Benevolent fire cooks our food, warms us, and gives us light in the darkness. Fire, the destroyer, burns uncontrollably and lays waste to all that stands in its way. Fire is also a purifier in both forms, benevolent and destructive. Death by fire or by being burned to death is one of the most feared ways to die, and yet, people willingly and happily have fire in their homes. Russian homes, in particular, faced with the long and bitterly cold winters, had large, powerful ovens for both cooking and heating. My home has strange proportions depending on my needs, but there is a great oven. I am a guardian of the underworld—it is part of my symbolism of being associated with winter and death The passage to the underworld must be guarded—and so it is by three priestesses and the oven itself—most people don't willingly venture into ovens, after all. So this young fool comes brashly to my house. He brings none of the traditional gifts as respectful offerings—no wine or honey or fruit or meat. He asks to be a man, and I tell him to appease the priestesses. Again, the fool has not been properly prepared, and he doesn't understand the ritual sex that is part of his transition to manhood. The priestesses all overlook this slight and still try to help him by trying to explain how to position himself in the oven to make the passage to the underworld so that he will not be burned and can return from his journey—a return that will make him a man. But he fails to do this for all three of the priestesses, and finally runs away—as much a child and a fool as when he came.

The priests hate the fact that people still tell my stories. Distorted as they are, one can, with the right lens, peel them back and see what is too scandalous for the poor Church Fathers to stomach. They plot my destruction. Silly fools. They do not know what I am. They do not know that they cannot kill me. They see a strange old woman with too long arms (a man's arms), but they do not know my power. They can try to send me to the underworld—but that is my place as much as the upper world. I cross between worlds. They cannot contain me. But they will try.

Though I knew the priest was trying to get me, it was the Spring Equinox again. So I went to the river and bathed. It was frightfully cold. But cleansing is part of the ritual. I had underestimated the old jackal. He had massed a group of angry villagers, and they came at me as I stepped out of the river.

"My God!" the priest exclaimed in shock. "W…what kind of demon are you?" The priest crossed himself and stepped back. "Beware," he bellowed, "it is an abomination," he announced to the crowd.

"No, I am not a demon. I am a merging of what can be—female and male, life and death, heaven and earth," I said, trying to defend myself.

"Speak not of heaven, witch. You are un-natural, and we cannot allow your contamination," spat the priest. "Bind her. And fire, ready a fire. The witch must burn!" he shrieked.

How fast they scurried to carry out his orders. Rough hands grabbed me, and my hands were tied behind my back. I couldn't believe that fat, old, lazy Tom could move so fast in his search for kindling, but he did, relieved that his own sins were being overshadowed by mine. People wouldn't look at me. I tried to speak, but then I was gagged. The pyre at the foot of a sapling Maple was assembled quicker than I thought possible. I was bound to the tree, and the priest brought the torch.

With demented glee, he took off the gag and said, "I condemn you to hell, witch," and lit the pyre. I could only imagine the sermons that would come out of this—scaring the faithful into blind obedience. Poor old women everywhere who could be accused of being witches— monsters, aberrations, freaks, like Baba Yaga. Only they are not Baba Yaga, but mortal women whose hair and flesh will burn—who will die in searing agony at the hands of small minded, intolerant men like this priest.

But I am Baba Yaga, and fire is one of my elements. The flames lapped up, and I simply crossed to the underworld. The poor priest and his followers—what would they do? Instead of their glorious execution—I just disappeared. No screams of unbearable agony, no smells of burning flesh. Just gone. I am sure they would run to my little house and try to torch that too. But my little house had already started walking away, into the sanctuary of the deep dark woods. It would find me when I crossed back. It always does.

CONTRIBUTORS

Jonathan Bracker's poems have appeared in *The New Yorker, Poetry Northwest, Writer's Digest*, and other periodicals; in several small press anthologies; and in seven small press collections. His *Concerning Poetry: Poems About Poetry* was published this year by the Upper Hand Press. He is the editor of *Bright Cages: The Selected Poems of Christopher Morley* (University of Pennsylvania Press: 1965), co-author with Mark Wallach of Christopher Morley (Twayne Press: 1976), and editor of *A Little Patch of Shepherd's-Thyme: Prose Passages of Thomas Hardy Arranged as Verse* (Moving Finger Press: 2013). Bracker has lived in San Francisco since 1973.

Michael Ceraolo is a 60-year-old retired firefighter/paramedic and active poet who has had two full-length books (*Euclid Creek*, from Deep Cleveland Press, and *500 Cleveland Haiku*, from Writing Knights Press) and numerous shorter-length books published, and has a third full-length book, *Euclid Creek Book Two*, forthcoming from unbound content press.

John W. Dennehy is an American novelist and short story writer. His novels include *Clockwork Universe* and *Pacific Rising*, and his short stories have appeared in *Dual Coast Magazine, Calliope, Typehouse Literary Magazine, Fiction on the Web, The Stray Branch*, and many more. He studied Creative Writing at UNC Wilmington.

Alan Fleishman has previously published three novels, a novella, and eight short stories. An historical novel, *A Fine September Morning*, has been his most successful work to date. Prior to becoming an author, Fleishman was a senior corporate executive, a strategic marketing consultant, and an officer in the U.S. Army. Today he and his wife Ann live with their Siberian cat, Pasha, high on a hill overlooking San Francisco Bay. For more information, visit: www.alanfleishman.com.

Louis Gallo's work has appeared or will shortly appear in *Wide Awake* *in the Pelican State* (LSU anthology), *Southern Literary Review, Fiction Fix, Glimmer Train, Hollins Critic,, Rattle, Southern Quarterly, Litro, New Orleans Review, Xavier Review, Glass: A Journal of Poetry, Missouri Review, Mississippi Review, Texas Review, Baltimore Review, Pennsylvania Literary Journal, The Ledge, storySouth, Houston Literary Review, Tampa Review, Raving Dove, The Journal (Ohio), Greensboro Review,*and many others. Chapbooks include *The Truth Change, The Abomination of Fascination, Status Updates and The Ten Most Important Questions.* He is the founding editor of the now defunct journals, *The Barataria Review* and *Books: A New Orleans Review.* He teaches at Radford University in Radford, Virginia.

Susie Gharib is a graduate of the University of Strathclyde with a Ph.D. on the work of D.H. Lawrence. Her fiction and poetry have appeared in Adelaide Literary Magazine. She is a lover of Nature and enjoys swimming.

Kevin Harris lives in Silver Spring, MD, and is currently a writer/editor and government contractor with the Food and Drug Administration. With a journalism and sociology background, Kevin has more than 20 years of copy editing, proofreading, and writing experience combined. His previous short stories include "Fire" was published in the now-defunct *Skylark,* a Purdue University Calumet, in the Fall 1998 edition and "The Trail" published in February 2018 in *The Long Story 36.* He's written several news and feature articles for the Maryland *Gazette* newspaper in Southern Prince George's County as well as articles highlighting to achievements of corrections professionals for the American Correctional Association's flagship magazine *Corrections Today.* Kevin has also written three novel manuscripts of which his first one is currently being reviewed and edited by a professional editor.

Rob Luke is a graduate of the M.F.A in Creative Writing Program from Minnesota State, Mankato. He teaches English at Delano High School in Minnesota. He lives on Lake Minnewashta, near the town of Excelsior, Minnesota, with his wife, Sara.

Tom McFadden was born in 1945 in Lancaster, Pennsylvania and met his wife, from Hershey, when both were journalism students at Penn State. They now live in Austin, Texas, where they have raised three daughters. Tom's writing has appeared in such venues as *Poetry Ireland Review, Poetry Salzburg Review, London Grip, Galway Review, Voices Israel, JAMA, Seattle Review, Hawaii Pacific Review, South Carolina Review, Portland Review and California Quarterly.*

Andrew Alexander Mobbs released his debut poetry collection, *Strangers and Pilgrims* (Six Gallery Press), in 2013. His poems have appeared in *Deep South Magazine, New Plains Review, Ghost Ocean Magazine, The Round, After Happy Hour Review, Bayou Magazine,* and elsewhere, and he was nominated for a Pushcart Prize in 2014. His academic publications include an article in *English Teaching Forum*. He co-edits the online literary journal *Nude Bruce Review.*

Kathleen Murphey is an associate professor of English at Community College of Philadelphia. She writes academic papers for presentation at regional and national conferences and fiction. She has turned one of her alternative fairy tales, "P Pan and Beyondland," into a play which will be performed as part of the Philadelphia Fringe Arts Festival, September 2018. More information about her work can be found at her website, www.kathleenmurphey.com.

Timothy Robbins teaches ESL. He has a B.A. in French and an M.A. in Applied Linguistics. He has been a regular contributor to Hanging Loose since 1978. His poems have appeared in Three New Poets, Slant, Main Street Rag, Adelaide Literary Magazine, Off the Coast and others. His collection *Denny's Arbor Vitae* was published in 2017. He lives with his husband of twenty years in Kenosha, Wisconsin.

R. Joseph Rodríguez teaches in the Kremen School of Education and Human Development at California State University, Fresno. His conversations with contemporary American authors have appeared in a number of periodicals. Joseph serves as coeditor of *English Journal*, a publication of the *National Council of Teachers of English*. Catch him virtually @escribescribe or via email: rjrodriguez@csufresno.edu.

Robert Ronnow's most recent poetry collections are *New & Selected Poems: 1975-2005* (Barnwood Press, 2007) and *Communicating the Bird* (Broken Publications, 2012). Visit his web site at www.ronnow-poetry.com.

Kobina Wright is an American writer, artist, actress and language creator. She is a native of California, and received her B.A. from California State University, Fullerton. She is the creator of the Hodaoa-Anibo language and co-creator of nuler styled poetry.

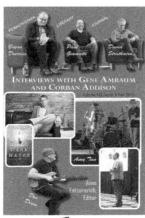

Pennsylvania Literary Journal

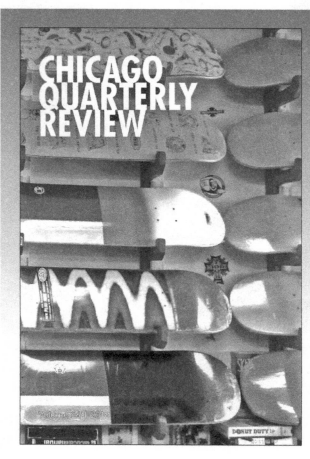

Fiction

Poetry

Art

Translations

Essays

Work from our pages recently has been chosen for *Best American Short Stories*, the *O. Henry Prize Stories*, and the *Pushcart Prize Anthology*.

chicagoquarterlyreview.com

CPSIA information can be obtained
at www.ICGtesting.com
Printed in the USA
BVHW031356141219
566688BV00001B/28/P

9 781681 144757